KV-512-880

INSPIRATION IN
LEADERSHIP

INSPIRATION IN
LEADERSHIP

Art and Science

Inspiration and Perspiration

Finding Balance

*A Personal Journey in Sales Leadership
and Sales Management*

KEVIN G. ISAAC

Copyright © 2024 by Inspiration in Leadership Ltd.

All rights reserved. No part of this book may be reproduced or used in any manner without written permission of the copyright owner except for the use of quotations in a book review. For more information, contact: info@inspirationinleadership.com

First Paper Back Edition: 2024

Book design by PublishingPush

978-1-80541-162-8 (hardcover)
978-1-80541-160-4 (paperback)
978-1-80541-161-1 (ebook)

www.inspirationinleadership.com

———————————

To my wonderful wife, Marinella, who has been the steadfast rock in my life, supporting me and always putting the family first while I was away for much of the time running businesses and investing in people. And to my two sons, Joshua and Jordan, who I know deserved more of my time but have grown into wonderful men, mostly due to my incredible wife! I hope my heart and character shine through these pages, and I dedicate them to you.

CONTENTS

Purpose of This Book   xiii

About the Author   xvii

**CHAPTER 1 PLOTTING THE COURSE AND GETTING THE
            BASICS RIGHT**   **1**

Common Sense Is Not Common   2

Are You Good or Are You Lucky?   3

Are You Process-Driven or Results-Driven?   4

Courage   6

Are You *Sharing*, *Shielding*, or *Filtering*?   9

Importance of First- and Second-Line Management   10

Goal Setting: Input and Output   11

Loyalty over Ability   11

Ego   12

Focus on What You Can Control   14

Fail Fast   15

CHAPTER 2 THE SCIENCE   17

What Does Success Look Like?   19

The Foundations and the Facts   20

Planning Organizational Structures   25

Opening Offices and Establishing Entities   30

Competencies and Role Types   32

Hiring   35

Using the STAR Method in Hiring   38

Roles and Responsibilities   39

Management Playbook and Cadence   40

Setting Expectations   44

Building a Quarterly Cadence Wheel by Week   44

Building a Quarterly Interdepartmental Calendar   47

Building a Management Playbook and Communication Strategy   47

The Critical Few for Sales   50

Aligning to the 6 Ps   51

Setting Expectations for Role Types and Players   54

Balance vs. Bureaucracy   55

Inspection   56

QBRs (Quarterly Business Reviews)   60

Format and Cadence   *60*

Root Cause Analysis   63

Failure, Gap Plans, and Performance Management   64

Performance Improvement Plans   66

Decisions Are Your Legacy   67

Deal and Account Reviews   68

Leading and Lagging Indicators   71

Developing First-Line Managers   72

Pipeline Generation   75

CHAPTER 3   THE ART   **77**

Finding Balance   80

The Basics   81

Attitude Affects Altitude   82

First, Be a Giver   82

Listening   84

    Weekly 1:1 Calls with Your Direct Reports   *86*
    Skip-Level Calls with Key People in Your Team   *87*
    Brown Bag Lunches   *87*
    Surveys   *88*
    Powerful Questions   *89*

Communication and Direction Setting   90

The Leadership Spine   91

Change Management   92

    Logic and Transparency Come First   *93*
    Building the Plan   *93*
    Executing on the Change Management Plan   *94*

Annual Communication Plans   95

Half-Year Communication 97

Quarterly Communication 98

    1. A Post-Quarter Note   *98*
    2. A Quarterly All-Hands Call   *99*
    3. A Quarterly Managers' Call   *100*
    4. Monthly   *101*
    5. Weekly   *102*

Global and Regional Differentiation 103

Embrace Diversity 106

Collaboration 108

Inspirational Leadership 109

Mission 110

Creativity 113

Difficult Conversations 115

Gut Feel 117

What then *How* then *Who* 118

Insight: Tell Me What I Don't Know! 119

Balance 121

Offsite Meetings, Events, and Reward Trips 122

    Offsite Meetings   *122*
    Ethics in Offsite Meetings   *123*
    Team Building at Offsites   *124*
    Reward Trips   *126*
    Planning Reward Trips   *126*

Building an Effective Kickoff Event 129

    Location   *130*

Building the Theme 131
What You Want to Achieve 131
The Curriculum and Order of Events 132
When Should I Run My Kickoff? 133

Inspiring Leaders   134

*Inspiration and Manipulation: Two Sides of the
    Same Coin? 134*
The Elements of Inspirational Leadership 136
Can Inspirational Leadership Be Learned? 138

CHAPTER 4 PERSPIRATION, NOT INSPIRATION   141

Getting It Done   142

Important Weekly Repetitive Tasks 143
Prioritized Cadence Activities 146
Calendared Activities 146

"The Ideas Factory Is Closed"   147

Delegation   148

Burnout   149

Grit   150

Recommended Reading   152

PURPOSE OF THIS BOOK

This book is designed for leaders—both seasoned sales leaders *and* senior leaders who are interested in building a great, results-oriented culture. For sales leaders in new roles, I hope to offer a helpful perspective, a view of the whole battlefield, and hopefully some assurance that what you are doing is right.

Sales leadership is a mix of art, science, inspiration, and hard, often repetitive, work—that is, perspiration. But as with many leadership positions, most sales leaders do not train for their roles. They are either promoted from a successful selling career or thrust, through corporate need, into a position where there is very little guidance that is practical and holistic. It is no wonder then that so many fail.

How many of us can identify with stories about challenging work environments? A tough boss, a culture that lacks trust, a manager with "favorite" employees, a senior leader with no empathy. Any one of these dysfunctions can result in incredible hardship. On your own leadership journey then, I ask a simple question:

"What culture will you build, and how
do you want to be remembered?"

I believe that we all enter leadership positions with the intention of doing well and making a positive contribution to our results, our culture, and our environment. But like hope, intention is not a strategy. In sales, winning is the obvious objective, but along the way, *how* we win and the *people we help or hurt* not only build our legacy—they can determine the extent of our achievement and the repeatability of our outcomes. I also hold firmly to the belief that management can be learned if you are prepared to invest time and effort, and leadership can be learned if you care deeply for people.

There are many facets of sales leadership roles to consider, and this book is broken down into specific segments so that you can choose which parts will benefit you the most. The title of the book speaks not only to a kind of "alchemy" of successful sales leadership, it also provides helpful structure to the book, which is broadly organized into three major chapters: *Science*, *Art*, and *Perspiration*.

We'll start with the *science* of great leadership and management and then delve into what I call the *art*. In my experience, successful leaders skillfully balance these elements and as a result are appreciated (even loved) and respected in equal measure. It is difficult to maintain this balance while being a boss, a friend, a disciplinarian, and a coach, depending on the circumstance. Not everyone is going to like you all the time, but your job is to ensure that they at least respect you. As we begin, I will share a few foundational elements of leadership and people management.

The sharp-eyed reader will have noted that inspiration, which is in the book title, does not get its own chapter. That's because I wanted to weave this critical element into the overall fabric of the book. In addition, I will cover some insights on inspirational leadership within the *Art* chapter, where I believe there are some specific perspectives that need to be considered.

Finally, there is a thinking process called "the ladder of inference."[1] (It is often called the ladder of assumption.) Simply put, the lack of all the facts sometimes leads, or "ladders up," to the wrong conclusions or resultant actions. If you are currently sitting in judgment of your sales team or are about to fire someone for not making their number, please take a moment to consider your data and whether there may be other contributing factors. Sales is a system of systems. It is hard, and the results are binary, but the inputs are not.

And sales leaders need all the help they can get.

---

1   Developed by Chris Argyris in 1970

ABOUT THE AUTHOR

I consider myself a very fortunate person. An optimist but also a realist, I am not a massive risk taker, though I have certainly had to seize opportunities when they presented themselves.

I was born in Zimbabwe (then Rhodesia) and spent my formative years living in a country at war until, at the age of 14, independence was won, shifting our world to a new reality. Unencumbered by the turmoil of my formative years, I was left with a sense of duty, care, and overarching service. During my later teens and early twenties, the country experienced a massive diaspora, which delivered to people like me the opportunity to grow faster and learn through necessity. I am so grateful for these formative years, for the richness of the experience, and for the opportunities I would never have had otherwise.

Sales has always been in my DNA, and while I began my career in banking, I really found my purpose once I settled into sales roles. Within five years of leaving banking, I was the general manager and CEO of an IT distribution startup, which counted among its partners Microsoft, Motorola, U.S. Robotics, and Symantec. In 1998, when a Microsoft executive asked me how I had achieved such incredible growth, I honestly couldn't answer him; I believed I was "lucky." I also believed that lightning never struck the same place twice, but over the years, repeatable processes and understanding the "playbook" delivered many successes to me, leaving a legacy of successful quarters and years as well as many great people I proudly call friends today.

In those early years I coined a phrase:

Success is due to people, people are driven by relationships, and relationships require commitment and effort.

I mention this because nothing is possible without great people and a commitment to one another that can overcome challenging realities. The single largest lesson I have learned in my 30-year career as a leader is that people are the single biggest influencer of success. Treat others with respect and empathy, be timely and open in your communication, lead with trust and good will, and little will stand in your way.

In 1999, I was fortunate to join Symantec a few months after John W. Thompson came on as CEO from IBM. It was still a relatively small business, under 1,000 people, and in my new-hire training I still remember John explaining to us that the company was a "diamond in the rough," one that we had the incredible opportunity to polish. My 18 years at Symantec were a journey of discovery, growth, and success, and I consider myself beyond fortunate to have served with such a great group of people in an amazing culture.

I have also been fortunate to work in some of the world's most important cybersecurity software companies, serving as SVP of EMEA at Symantec, Sophos, and Forcepoint, and as CRO at Forcepoint, where we had the opportunity to integrate numerous companies and mold them into one culture and one sales motion. The journey has had its highs and its lows, and I am grateful to all the people who walked the path with me and built such a solid foundation to help me write this book.

CHAPTER ONE

Plotting the Course and
Getting the Basics Right

Common Sense Is Not Common

In the mid-1990s, while working as the sales and marketing director of a plastics company, I was on the factory floor with my CEO looking at a large, six-color flexographic printer. The print run had been a disaster because the new printing manager had mistakenly added cyan ink where the magenta was meant to go. Now, I was a "sales guy" with no experience in production, but I immediately saw the error. My CEO smiled at me and said, "Common sense is not common. Make no assumptions and communicate well." Those words have stuck with me.

Much of this book is focused on the process of improvement, with stories and best practices that relate to people, from junior managers to senior execs, and businesses, from startups to large organizations. I hope to provide context and insight through my experiences—including some mistakes that I learned from and some that provided insight for others.

One such experience was at a team offsite after a particularly successful year. One of the vice presidents who ran another region came up to me and said, "What is your secret?" I knew him well, and my intuition was to ask him a simple question: "How often do you talk to your people informally, just one-on-one?" He was surprised at the question, and I went on to explain that most days, no matter where I was in the world that week, I would take 30 minutes, wander around the office, perch on the corner of someone's desk, and ask them how they were. In these safe, uncomplicated moments, I probably learned the most. I also inspired a lot of trust through the one-on-one relationships that developed over time. I believe that these simple "common sense" acts of communication are key to building foundational success.

Are You Good or Are You Lucky?

For most of the first two decades of this century, I worked for Symantec, an American software company that specializes in cyber security, in roles ranging from director to senior vice president. The company grew considerably in those years, and as it did, our global leadership provided training and resources to help us all grow with it. To facilitate that growth, Jay Tyler, a talented "change agent," was brought in to help train, coach, and mentor us. Jay, who remains a good friend to this day, spoke these words to me after I had delivered north of 150 percent of plan: "Are you good or are you lucky?" Jay had a unique way of pushing his students' buttons, and as I was frankly offended. I had to decide quickly whether I would get angry or choose to see the wisdom in his question and open myself up to the possibility that I may just learn something.

The truth is that luck plays a large part in most of our lives, and accepting that simple fact can be humbling. The famous golfer Gary Player said, "The more I practice, the luckier I get," and in this wisdom (and the words of Jay Tyler) lay a simple truth: Regardless of the results you deliver today, you need a repeatable system that is based on best practices and solid, operationalized frameworks that you work hard to constantly improve. Being good at your job means being successful, being able to *repeat* success, and then *define* how you did it—*every single time*.

What being good does *not* require is that you have all the ideas or be the smartest person in the room. Success is normally attained when people collaborate, listen, share, and then team up to deliver incredible outcomes. This may seem fundamental, but in Sales—where, let's face it, "type A" personalities are the norm and arrogance and self-aggrandizement are not uncommon—the people who understand it as a principle are prepared to submit to wisdom and to learn. These people have the potential to become titans in their areas of expertise and see their "luck" magnified through good will, teamwork, and hard work.

Are You Process-Driven or Results-Driven?

Over the past two decades I have been fortunate to work for some great leaders—people I'm grateful and proud to call friends. As the multinational businesses we worked for grew and matured, we realized that we needed to more clearly understand how we had achieved our strategic outcomes. As a result, we implemented processes to build plans that helped our teams understand the part we all played in delivering those outcomes.

In other words, we became decidedly process-driven.

However, many I have worked with over the years would have understandably answered the subject question with an enthusiastic "Results-driven!" Such a person might be a team leader whose key goal was to grow net-new customers by 30 percent. For this person, failing to meet this goal meant facing the wrath of a manager. In this scenario, the goal could be stated as "hit the target" and the process as "aim well." Hardly a formula for improvement when the only option for refining the process is "aim better."

And if the threat of a dressing down by an angry manager at quarter's end was not enough of a process bogeyman, witness the average CRM system, where opportunities are probably not up to date, sales stages are fuzzy (or wrong), and the qualification process is sketchy, at best. Then there's the unfortunate but reliable friction between Marketing and Sales about MQLs (marketing qualified leads) and SALs (sales accepted leads) and management's inability to forecast because Sales are not updating their forecasting tool properly. Any of this sound familiar? What about the channel and account planning process and the interlock between Sales and Marketing? Can you go back and look at the territory plan of a given region from two years ago? How is Finance meant to set the goals for next year? Worse still, how can you debate with Finance what the numbers should be for next year if you have no foundational science or evidence to back up your position?

These all-too-common scenarios are a big part of the reason most sales leaders are results-driven. Attention to detail is difficult and taking time to update records and "serve the data" can seem wasteful and counterintuitive to sales professionals under heavy time constraints and revenue targets. But a lack of attention to detail and process not only makes repeatable execution somewhere between difficult and impossible, it prevents us from being able to interrogate a plan to learn what decisions were made and why, and how we might make better decisions going forward.

Not all falls at the feet of sales leadership, however. Pressure from the board, the CEO, and the CFO often results in unreasonable requests for planning and data, pivots in execution, and turmoil due to unexpected and unplanned requests for information. For the CXOs reading this book, please remember the adage: When you kick a pebble off the mountaintop, you cause an avalanche below.

I don't think we should see this as an excuse in sales, but I do accept that turmoil and change often lead to sales staff focusing on the most important work of closing deals (i.e., the results) *despite* the process. The next step in this dysfunction is usually when a quarter or a target is missed, which usually results in extra bureaucracy and process raining down on an already injured team. But while attempting to address performance issues with more bureaucracy may create a feel-good story for the executives and the board, this rarely addresses the root cause.

If some form of rule change or additional bureaucracy is absolutely necessary due to a missed target or some error, then consider where you may also be able to "trim" a little to avoid a net increase in red tape. There are likely to be some inefficiencies baked into your process that you can remove, and doing so will show commitment to your team and support for the work they're doing. Simply adding to the list of rules is rarely the best solution.

So, are you process-driven or results-driven?

The best answer to the question is actually *both*. Without repeatable results, there's no business, and without process, repeatable results are unsustainable. But to achieve a healthy process/results balance, everyone in the sales organization needs to buy into this, and management must deliver a predictable, no-surprises environment to enable Sales to feel safe and supported. How much more productive do you think your salespeople could be in the field if, as they engage in battle, they're no longer having to watch their backs, worried that a missed target will bring automatic hellfire from management or senior leadership? To earn a place on this field, however, Sales must commit to a process "fitness regime" where training, measurement, best practices, and clear KPIs all play key roles.

Courage

Leadership and being responsible for a business are not for the faint of heart. From challenging your boss to disciplining your team to firing a colleague you feel personally close to—when you've prepared yourself for every contingency, sometimes courage is the only thing that will get you through.

In my first board meeting as a CRO, one of the board members leaned across the table and said, "Do you own the number? When will you be able to look me in the eye and tell me you have got it?" For those of you in similar roles, you know what I am talking about. While you are winning, courage is a simple word that can be used flippantly, almost like a weapon. It is only when things are really hard that the word has real meaning.

Courage, according to Oxford English Dictionary, is "the ability to do something dangerous, or to face pain or opposition, without showing fear." I prefer this idiom: *To have the courage of your convictions is to be brave enough to do what you feel to be right.*

Years ago, I worked as the general manager of a large manufacturing plant in Zimbabwe. One day, the chairman of the board coached me, saying, "This Friday, fire yourself, and spend the weekend 'unemployed.' Think about all the things you wish you had done a little differently, then on Monday morning, rehire yourself. List all the things the guy last week should have done or didn't do right, and then focus on that list." Every day we have the opportunity to change our future. I often coach my teams to visualize the end of the quarter and the end of the fiscal year. What do you see, and what will you regret? Right now, you can change and adjust the outcome. But it takes courage.

It may sound simplistic, but one of the hardest things to learn in business—and one that takes the most courage—is making decisions (see section *Making Decisions*). To be sure, having the facts and being able to form your own opinion on a subject before making an important decision are much more preferrable to being caught out and relying on raw instinct and experience. Courage is also anchored in your convictions and in taking a view on something and seeing it through. I strongly recommend a mentor, someone who has been in your position and can prepare you for the questions and challenges you are about to confront so that you have time to come to your own conclusions. In one of my early career sales leadership roles, I was at a staff offsite meeting where we delved into the P2 (performance over potential) metrics of our direct reports. The discussion quickly moved to the lower-performing staff members, and before I had time to process, we made decisions that I was not prepared to make, decisions that had real consequences for real people. If instead I had demanded more time, I would have been able to think through and then argue my true feelings, potentially influencing those decisions in a different way. But in the moment, I didn't have the courage to say, "I'm not sure," or, "I need more time to look at the data."

As a sales leader, you should make every decision with thoughtful consideration of the information (and opinions) on hand, the impacts and outcomes of your decision, and the courage to face them. The importance of careful decision-making in leadership in general, and sales leadership in particular, cannot be understated. You may, for example, offhandedly agree on the date for compliance training only to realize afterwards that it is at the quarter end.

Another good example of the importance of thoughtful, informed, and timely decision-making is a situation where a leader, lacking the courage to confront an awkward or painful performance issue, delays putting an individual on a needed performance improvement plan. As a result, the individual is eventually fired. The company now faces lost sales revenue from that employee and is also hit with a lawsuit for wrongful termination based on their failure to properly follow process. This may sound hypothetical, but it is more common than you may think.

Even with careful consideration, wise counsel from trusted advisors, and data all playing their part, courage is still vital in sales leadership. Hard decisions must be made and should not be put off. A CEO (and friend) I worked for often said to me, "Now is the point of least risk. Make your decision quickly before other factors and time increase your risk." Quite frankly, after most of the hard decisions I have made (most regarding people), the only real question afterward has been, "What took you so long?"

Are You *Sharing, Shielding,* or *Filtering?*

In a recent conversation, a global sales leader shared some of the frustrations he was experiencing as his company went through immense change. The process had revealed to him that there are three types of leaders: those who *share* their challenges, those who *shield* their problems, and those who *filter* their challenges with staff.

Conventional wisdom says that we should always be honest with our people and share our challenges, but CEOs will tell you that one of an executive leader's most important roles is "chief cheerleader"—the eternal optimist, the one who always says it can be done. So, how do we square these conflicting approaches? In my experience, shielding important information from your team, regardless of how bad it is, only delays the inevitable. It could even foster mistrust, causing your team to question whether they are getting the whole truth. When you shield your team, they will not understand the seriousness of an issue and may, in ignorance, focus on objectives that dilute the company's ability to address that issue. Trusting in your team's resilience in the face of challenging news, and in their willingness to follow you regardless, will foster more courageous communication and inspire them to take up the flag.

I do not believe that a CEO's role as "chief optimist" necessarily conflicts with being absolutely honest. The leader's role is to find the right balance, trusting that the team will not only understand strategic challenges but even use them to steel their resolve in the field. As Simon Sinek tweeted, "Transparency doesn't mean sharing every detail. Transparency means providing the context for the decisions we make."

Importance of First- and Second-Line Management

For the uninitiated, first-line management is a term for those who directly manage individual contributors within an organization. Second-line managers manage the first-line managers.

Regardless of the size of your sales organization, business is led through detail—those vital few metrics at the most basic level that give you the most leverage in results—and through a great first-line management culture and process. When I became a vice president at Symantec, my first focus was the first-line managers, from their day-to-day activities to their core competencies and what they believed (or what I coached them to focus on, trust, and value) to be important to the business. We built specific training modules for them and explained to them that they were pivotal to our sales organization's success. Over my first nine months, every manager attended simple online courses on coaching, goal setting, leadership, emotional intelligence, and decision-making.

The work we did in those months turned my group of first- and second-line managers into an integrated, functioning, and optimistic team who seized opportunities and began to follow a common set of goals, objectives, and processes. We then began to build dashboards on operating cadence and leaderboards for CRM hygiene to "gamify" their success. The results were outstanding.

Goal Setting: Input and Output

Part of our journey in developing our first line—and in realizing that process was just as important as results—was moving from lagging indicators to leading indicators. I will cover this more in the *Science* chapter of the book, but suffice here to say that if your company's goal is to deliver top-line growth in new logo accounts, measuring the sales team on new logo bookings (a lagging indicator) will not necessarily deliver the desired outcome. The leading indicator, what you should be measuring, may be the number of cold calls a rep makes to new customers.

Taking a goal and reducing it to its single most basic input, like a phone call, can be the difference between inertia and changing the direction your team is traveling in. Again, details count, and as a leader, while it is important to focus on what the board wants, getting to the most basic metrics will give you the ability to determine which teams and which activities are most likely to drive results. For more on this I recommend *Cracking the Sales Management Code*[2] by Jason Jordan and Michelle Vazzana.

Loyalty over Ability

You see it all the time in business: Leaders who reward loyalty over ability, building teams and systems that eventually—inevitably—crumble under the weight of dysfunction and incompetence.

Boards or CEOs must eventually make decisions to remove these leaders, and when this happens the structure tends to crumble like a house of cards. Great teams are built around values of results and performance, and with an understanding that loyalty comes in the form of "air cover."

2   [Citation]

When the leaders who build these teams move on, their teams are much better equipped to survive the change. I was particularly proud when I left Symantec after more than 17 years, soon after the merger with Bluecoat. Almost every one of my management team remained in their positions in the new organization and went on to contribute incredibly in the following years, a great testament to a solid legacy. We should all strive for this and judge leadership not just on contemporaneous results but also on the outcomes following a leader's departure.

Ego

While the word "ego" often carries negative connotations, a healthy ego is necessary to be successful. Knowing who you are and having the self-confidence to interact with people, make decisions, and execute are bottom-line requirements in business leadership. A challenge we often face in Sales, however, are managers whose over-inflated egos are not justified by their capabilities and outcomes.

Self-awareness and a willingness to receive feedback are key in any high-performing leadership team, and coaching and training are essential in developing these traits. When team members exhibit challenging behaviors, leadership and help should be within reach to assist. The last thing you want is for someone to fail because they didn't receive help with a challenging behavior, perhaps one they were unaware of.

During my career we used various tools to help our managers grow as leaders. One brilliant resource was an independent 360 assessment.[3] Because it was directed from outside the company and completely confidential, the assessment created an environment of trust for the team

3   We used an excellent product from Zenger Folkman.

to explore who they were. This process worked because it provided the survey subjects invaluable feedback from people outside the company, including customers and previous colleagues. Learning how they were perceived was quite powerful, and coaches could then take the survey recipient, or even entire teams, through the often ego-challenging feedback, helping them take constructive steps to make improvements.

The Johari Window[4] (Figure 1) technique is another tool I benefitted from early in my leadership journey. It helped me better understand my relationship with myself and uncovered areas within my personality that were unknown to me or where others may have had a perspective

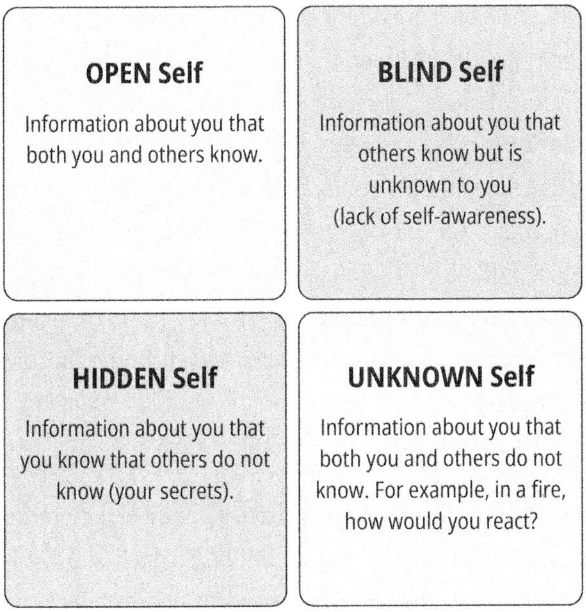

OPEN Self

Information about you that both you and others know.

BLIND Self

Information about you that others know but is unknown to you (lack of self-awareness).

HIDDEN Self

Information about you that you know that others do not know (your secrets).

UNKNOWN Self

Information about you that both you and others do not know. For example, in a fire, how would you react?

FIGURE 1 The Johari Window

---

4   The Johari Window was created by psychologists Joseph Luft (1916–2014) and Harrington Ingham (1916–1995).

about me that I was unaware of. This tool was put to good use in a half-day workshop I attended at a business I had recently joined. I left the room, and my HR leader asked my direct reports to debate each quadrant and their perceptions of me—my strengths, weaknesses, and areas for improvement. After an hour, I was invited back and offered feedback, with the opportunity to discuss, explain, and learn. It was a powerful experience, one that gave my team a chance to share their candid perceptions of me while giving me an opportunity to course correct or clarify expectations or intentions.

Focus on What You Can Control

When I was a new vice president at a global software company, my CEO called a vice presidents' meeting near our company headquarters. This was soon after Michael Jackson's sad demise, and when we all arrived, "Man in the Mirror" was playing. It was a poignant moment when the CEO talked about our own ability to look in the mirror and evaluate our performance, our teamwork, and what we were personally focused on. As with every company, there is always the risk of blaming our failure on another department or analyzing another group to determine how they could do *their* jobs better, but our focus should be on *our* roles, taking responsibility for *our* execution, playing as a team, and focusing on what we can control.

The dark side of this is passive-aggressive behavior, where we not only stop focusing on our own execution but begin gaslighting our peers or working against them because we have lost perspective in how to win as a team. It often starts with criticizing or questioning another person or department by a team member who may be looking for validation or for a way to assuage their own failure. Team members who are insecure or struggling with their own value or relevance are particularly at risk of this behavior, and if it is not nipped in the bud and rooted out, it can develop into a cancer that destabilizes the whole team. (See Figure 15 later in the book for a visual on a couple of the forms passive-aggressive behavior can take.)

Encouraging your teams to focus on what they can control is so much more than just helping them become better at what they do. It is about understanding the dynamics of teams, encouragement, trust, and shared respect. (See introduction to *Art* chapter.)

Fail Fast

> *"Avoid having your ego so close to your position that*
> *when your position falls, your ego goes with it."*
>
> – COLIN POWELL

I am sure you've heard the phrase "fail fast"—probably many times. But how many people are able to actually do this? As I write this book, I am witnessing an incredible number of layoffs in the information technology sector, and I recently heard someone say, "Wow, they've made a huge mistake in letting that person go!" My perspective is slightly different. If a business gets to a point where a workforce correction of more than ten percent becomes necessary, there are likely endemic problems that have not been addressed in a continuous, systematic, and focused way. The result is the need for an "event" like a major reduction in force.

Ideas are created, plans are adjusted, the business grows, and people "disappear" into the fabric of the organization. Spans of control become diluted, and projects take on a life of their own. As costs mount and time pressures increasingly exacerbate challenges, problems that should be easy to fix aggregate until more senior staff are required to oversee change. When this happens, oftentimes your decision-making power as a senior leader can be removed in favor of others who are tasked with executing on things you should have had better control over.

Having logic and clarity of thought to know when a pet project is failing or when you are too emotionally attached to a plan to order its demise requires a willingness to listen and take input from those around you and a steadfast determination to stop the things that are failing before someone else does it for you.

Plotting a course and getting the basics right is not an event—it is an ongoing, evolving process that informs many areas of endeavor, both in business and in life. Consistently executing on the principles laid out in this chapter—the "basics"—will help you build the foundations of your brand and your business, while also providing some excellent life skills along the way.

CHAPTER TWO

The Science

In Moscow, in 2011, after a particularly successful quarter on the heels of several before it, my HR business partner asked me what we were doing to achieve such impressive repeatable success. His question stuck with me, and on my flight back to Dubai I began noodling on the "science" of what we were doing to achieve remarkable things. Success can be—and usually is—fleeting, so how were we able to repeat it, quarter after quarter. I realized that our science boiled down to a process, an understanding of the inputs required to achieve the desired outputs, and a set of principles for delivering the best traction. We then built a set of models or algorithms around how we made decisions on head count, opened new offices, measured performance, and compared different teams, all by way of ensuring that we were able to ignite the competitive spirit within the sales team and quickly identify best practices or areas for improvement.

Over the ensuing months and years, we built and refined a set of key principles, including measures and leading indicators that would help us deliver consistently outstanding results. We realized that we could not focus on everything (at least not at once or in a short period of time), so we distilled the most important levers for success down to a vital few KPIs, the key performance indicators we needed to carefully curate to align to the results we were after and the company's overall mission. We then reduced these KPIs to the simplest tasks that became the building blocks for great outcomes. I named this concise planning process the 6 Ps. (We'll cover the 6 Ps in detail later in the chapter.)

The foundational work in preparing a company's financial journey is just as important as the execution—or the journey itself. After all, once a course has been set and the "train has left the station," you better be sure the destination is achievable, as one of the greatest reasons for failure is setting the wrong expectations at the outset.

My approach has always been logical, from establishing a plan to gathering all the information to communicating exactly what is needed from each team member to delivering our visualized success. And while this may sound straightforward, the overwhelming scale of getting this right can be incredibly challenging. The challenges are always in the detail, and in everyone's willingness to listen, collaborate, and communicate prolifically.

On a recent call with an ex-colleague from our marketing team, we were talking about this book and she said, "In the early days, Sales didn't listen to us in Marketing because we spoke a different language and didn't understand their priorities." This is profound, and the potential for friction and frustration can be multiplied even more by all the other groups within an organization. Setting the tone from the top and creating uncomplicated priorities for everyone to get behind is foundational to overcoming cross-functional "language barriers" and establishing a highly successful team.

What Does Success Look Like?

One of the most basic requirements in any organization is being able to break down what success looks like to the people who will deliver it, from a macro-organizational perspective right down to what each team member needs to do to get an A in their annual review. Building a plan with clear KPIs based on the company's mission and vision and visualizing what success will look like in 12 and 36 months, these are the start to a planning process that you can then work backward from to decide what your team needs to do each quarter.

Items to consider include revenue, retention, growth, market share, customer satisfaction, cost, value, funding, hiring, and attrition, among others. You must boil down what is key to you and your organization and determine how to focus on the priorities *now* that will deliver the outcome you are visualizing.

Agility and vision are critical. If you are running a startup, I can almost guarantee that your plan will change and go through many iterations as you understand your customers' needs more thoroughly or realize you need to adjust your offering. If you are in a billion-dollar enterprise, you will know that market dynamics will change momentum just as frequently. Whatever the size of your business, it is vital to have both a plan and a clear vision of what success looks like so that you will know when you are deviating and how you are doing against your stated objectives.

Whether you are a CEO, CRO, or a leader of a sales team, take this approach and make it work for you, and you will find that the teams under your command will rally to the flag you fly, and energy will multiply through teamwork and shared vision.

The Foundations and the Facts

"If I had six hours to chop down a tree, I'd spend the first four hours sharpening the axe."

– ABRAHAM LINCOLN

Planning for great execution starts with understanding the basics. The data is important. It should include but not be limited to the following:

1. **Total Addressable Market (TAM)**: Normally, your leadership or investors will have a strong point of view on this. However, it is key to understand the *actual* market you can realistically address with

your solution (the addressable market), which is usually a subset of the TAM filtered by vertical industry, company size, geography, language, and other criteria. It is important to understand this and the potential areas of focus. Before you sign up to a number that you can own and deliver on, your analysis should include white space, coverage, and heat maps.

2. **Know Your Customer**: Before you can build and execute on a successful sales strategy, it is key to understand *how* a customer buys, *why* they buy, their perception of *value*, and their *expectations*. Demographics also play an important role. One of the startups I advise was pitching to companies with 50 employees—or at least that's what they thought. Digging into the analytics, we found that they had done a comparative technical analysis against competitors who supply products to companies with *250 employees*. The data further revealed that my client had been most successful in companies with an average of 20 employees. You can burn a lot of cash if you don't understand both your target "demographic" and your historical strengths.

Many startups I talk to say they know their ICP (ideal customer profile), but I encourage constant re-checking and listening to the market. ICPs change and they can change quickly.

3. **Plan Your Route to Market—Carefully**: There are ever more creative ways for businesses to reach their customers. If you're running a startup or beginning a new product line, be careful! Once you commit to a path, it will often define your future. For example, if you choose to use channel partners, understand that direct sellers may compete with them and potentially dilute your margins. This is an area where I strongly recommend strategic planning and counsel. One of the biggest challenges we had in the software industry

was paying both the channel and our salespeople on the same dollar booked. Assuming 35 percent margin for the channel, once you pay sales reps, managers, sales engineers, and channel sales, there is little profit left for the company. It is extremely difficult to wean the channel off a margin or a product line once you start down this road, and it is vital to plan for the future before making specific decisions or commitments.

4. **Productivity and Ramp Time**: This is the time it takes for a salesperson or team to become productive, and it is often underestimated. The last thing you want is for good salespeople to lose heart when their goals are unrealistic. Worse still is the risk of disappointing the CFO because you have made promises your team simply cannot deliver on. I have never met a finance person who wants to give you more time than you need, and setting the right expectations will take effort. Finance will always want it to be shorter and ROI projections to be sooner. You must set realistic expectations, or you will fail before starting.

   If salespeople are on what we call OTE (on target earnings), where perhaps 50 percent of their take-home is based purely on commission, you may also have to fund this as a guarantee for a period while that rep is learning the ropes. These discussions must be locked and built into financial projections before you begin the journey.

   Most enterprise sales ramp times will be in the region of six months. This can be shortened if a new salesperson is taking over an established territory or if they have brought with them a few existing relationships that have an imminent need. But if not, don't underestimate the ramp time, which includes product training, onboarding, and establishing a credible pipeline.

5. **Understand the Outcome Your CEO Requires**: Fifty percent growth is very different from 50 percent margin, and once you know what winning looks like to the board, you can work backward to create the building blocks required to deliver. This may be a tough conversation, and the CEO and CFO will probably be a little less excited by your budget requirements. Logic, meticulous data, and planning will be the key.

    In these situations, speaking truth to power is vital, and you will need courage to have deep conversations about what is possible. Just mind the extremes: If you are too conservative, you will not get the budget you need to execute, but if you simply accept the plan, you may run out of runway when the bookings plan does not stack up as expected. Honesty and a clear understanding of your opportunity are both vital along with your style of engagement and willingness to listen.

6. **Essential Key Performance Indicators (KPIs)**: As you distill the outcomes required with all your other data, you and your team should be able to arrive at a dozen or so key KPIs that, if you fanatically deliver on them, will move the needle. Consider my 6 Ps a north star here.

7. **Avoid Analysis Paralysis**: Despite the previous points, a team on the field that is busy talking and not "playing ball" will lose the game. Trust your gut, take advice from people you trust, and then lean in. Sales leadership requires courage and execution.

8. **Outsource Strategically**: There are two very different topics when discussing outsourcing in this context:

    a. **Outsourcing of Help in Building a Plan or a Key Strategy**. This should be done carefully and with a clear business reason for outsourcing such a strategic piece of work. Is it because you do not understand a specific market or geography? Or perhaps you need a certain skill or competency? Outsourcing is generally not something I advise when building a sales strategy. There may be areas where you can get expert assistance and I strongly recommend coaching for specific components of a plan, but once the plan is built, the owners of the business need to be 100 percent bought in. If the leaders of the business abdicate the responsibility for building the plan, odds are it will never be your plan.

b. **Outsourcing of a Sales Function in a Geographical Territory**. There are over 250 countries in the world today, but for large multinational software companies, 80 percent of business is generally conducted in about a dozen countries. Building a clearly understood core strategy for your company's key markets is essential. Focusing on where to play and how to win will make you more effective, and knowing where not to spend time is equally important. Regardless of your choices, your routes to market, and whether you outsource or subcontract, you will always own the strategy. Never forget this.

9. **Collaborate**: Board members and your management team want to help you. When you meet with them, remember that it is not a test of your intelligence and you do not have to be right all the time. In one board meeting I attended, the chairman challenged one of my strategies for investing in global alliances with large systems integrators, not because it was a bad idea, but because the time to value would be longer than the appetite of the investors. That was a brilliant insight that helped me to correct course before over-promising. Collaboration and understanding the end-to-end outcome from customer to employees to owners are foundational to success.

Planning Organizational Structures

One of the greatest challenges new sales leaders face is separating loyalty and friendships from the science and logic of building great teams. There is no excuse for creating a structure that is inefficient, overlapping in responsibilities, or too expensive due to the wrong ratios of roles resulting from clouded judgment.

I learned a simple methodology for the early stages of designing an organizational structure: First *what*, then *how*, then *who*. If you begin with *what* you are trying to achieve and move to the *how* without considering *who* you want in specific roles—and you are logical and honest with yourself in the process—you will create a much more appropriate structure when you add names to it. If you find that you cannot fit your favorite colleagues into the structure, perhaps some difficult decisions will ensue. Loyalty is important, but it comes with the very clear caveat that your primary responsibility is to do what is best for the company. If you take the easy path of hiring friends or allowing roles to become murky because you're afraid of jeopardizing loyalties, then you create unnecessary risk for everyone involved. It requires courage to explain what you are trying to do and why you are making certain decisions. These discussions need not be acrimonious, and when done with candor, empathy, and good logic, friendships can remain intact, no matter the outcome.

Restructuring is also particularly difficult. In 2015, when Symantec and Veritas separated into two multibillion-dollar companies, the job of separating teams and assigning roles was done exceptionally well. That said, we did make a few mistakes with some of the assignments simply because it was easier to choose an incumbent rather than running a full review and hiring process. At the end of the day, the choices you make on that whiteboard will determine your score on the field.

Take the time to think through tough decisions, don't abdicate the process, and understand that every decision—every piece of the puzzle—will come back to either help you or haunt you as the real work of execution takes place.

Ratios are a key tool you can use for building a great structure. In information technology sales teams, the best span of control, or ratio of managers to individual contributors, is 8:1 for field sales. A slightly higher number, up to 12:1, is possible in inside sales, but a total ratio of managers lower than seven risks inefficiency in the organization unless you are opening new markets where only a handful of staff work in a given location. In such a case, a manager with five or fewer employees should also carry some quota as a "player-manager." Be sure to document when player-managers are in your mix as your owners or board may get the wrong data in their algorithms when the different roles and spans of control are rolled up for review. Ratios of field, inside, technical, and channel are also critical and will depend on the type of organization and sales motion being implemented.

A key to this structure can also be found in commission structures and in whether the compensation plan is team-driven or highly individual. Salespeople can be paid for their work individually or for their work as a team. The organizational structure you build will play to these models, but how your company plans to pay their people should be calculated carefully to ensure the structure is set up properly. However, if you build a structure with too many people within a group, all paid on the same dollar sold, the resulting commissions could make your business unprofitable. A successful structure will always be a carefully curated, symbiotic ecosystem.

In my time leading sales teams, I have found it necessary to carefully manage the balance of power between the different teams that report to me to ensure that all have a seat at the table and feel equally relevant. I often say that the technical sales teams are the most important, and this is normally because their mix of skills is critical and hard to replicate, and they are less likely to comprise alpha personalities. Understanding the needs of the different groups and how to give them the attention they need is important if you wish to get the most out of the whole organization. In the past, I found myself spending more time with specific people or groups because I either liked them or found their energy to be additive to my own. But this is dangerous, as the outliers also need your time. Being self-aware and aware of all your teams' needs will keep your perspective balanced and your teams performing. If there are people you don't gravitate to, this could be a bigger problem and something you should address carefully before it grows.

You should also carefully consider your global structures. In my experience, franchising out an entire region to one individual may feel like the easiest thing to do, but reporting all functions through one person creates a single point of failure. A role with this much power situated a continent away can be extremely risky. My usual starting point is sales data. In most companies, America produces approximately 50 percent of worldwide sales, EMEA (Europe, Middle East, Africa) about 35 percent, and APJ (Asia Pacific, Japan) 15 percent or so. Key roles are therefore normally focused on the U.S. With this in mind, why would a company introduce unnecessary risk by implementing a general manager (GM) strategy for the U.S., where technical, channel, field, and inside sales report to a single U.S.-based GM?

One solution lies in teaming and cost of structures. In our EMEA organization in 2012, we moved from having a technical sales leader with direct line control and his own technical sales organization to a matrixed system where he had a dotted line to the team and gave country (regional) managers direct line control to technical sales. The

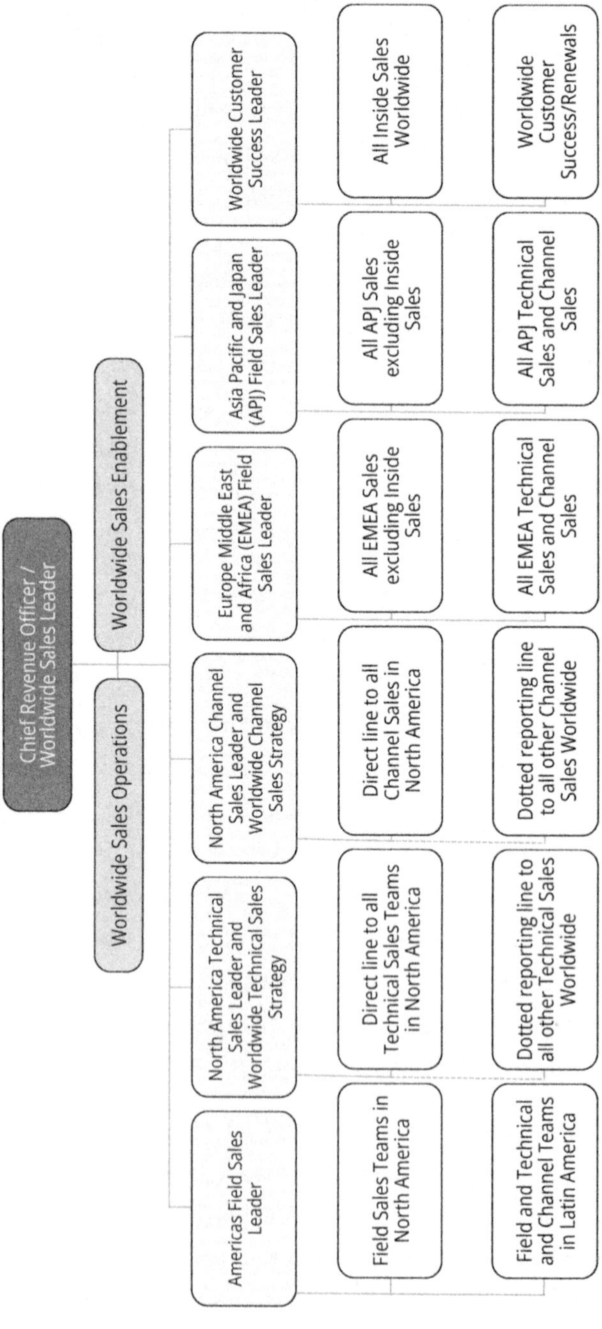

Chief Revenue Officer / Worldwide Sales Leader

Worldwide Sales Operations

Worldwide Sales Enablement

Americas Field Sales Leader
- Field Sales Teams in North America
- Field and Technical and Channel Teams in Latin America

North America Technical Sales Leader and Worldwide Technical Sales Strategy
- Direct line to all Technical Sales Teams in North America
- Dotted reporting line to all other Technical Sales Worldwide

North America Channel Sales Leader and Worldwide Channel Sales Strategy
- Direct line to all Channel Sales in North America
- Dotted reporting line to all other Channel Sales Worldwide

Europe Middle East and Africa (EMEA) Field Sales Leader
- All EMEA Sales excluding Inside Sales
- All EMEA Technical Sales and Channel Sales

Asia Pacific and Japan (APJ) Field Sales Leader
- All APJ Sales excluding Inside Sales
- All APJ Technical Sales and Channel Sales

Worldwide Customer Success Leader
- All Inside Sales Worldwide
- Worldwide Customer Success/Renewals

FIGURE 2 Example Sales Organizational Chart

savings in operational expenses and the improvement in alignment were significant, but it only worked because of outstanding technical leadership and a strong implementation of the RACI (responsible, accountable, consulted, and informed) matrix model.

Figure 2 illustrates my basic recommended structure for a global software sales organization.

The following examples illustrate how the RACI model supports this structure:

1. Channel or technical sales in North America, while directly managed by the channel or technical sales leader, need the approval or support of the North American sales leader before new hires or changes are signed off.
2. The channel or technical team in the rest of the world, while hired and directly managed by the local leader in theatre, still need approval from the worldwide channel or technical leadership to maintain the right tension and balance of power.
3. Budgets and head counts need shared vision from the different groups, including Finance and Operations, before being ratified to ensure the overall outcome is fit for purpose.

My perspective on making inside sales a separate function derives from the work these people do and the idea that their sales motion and work require a specific type of management and a different set of KPIs—things that most field sales leaders lack the cycles to focus on. Careful consideration of the work an individual does and the type of management they require is vital, and simply putting everyone into a bucket because they work in one office or one country makes no sense when considering how to execute effectively against specific competencies.

Opening Offices and Establishing Entities

The process of establishing an entity or opening an office is straightforward. Start by uncovering any hidden costs around ongoing fiduciary requirements and compliance. When we were expanding our worldwide operations, we built an algorithm to detail what we deemed a minimum viable group in any given location, including Sales, Technical, and Channel. The algorithm then calculated the running cost of the office, the admin burden, and the fully loaded people costs to determine a break-even sales revenue number we had to hit before we could open an entity or an office. Just the extra management burden of having another site can increase cost and complexity. Do you hire a manager for three people, or do you manage them from a remote location? Better still, can you service the region with an inside sales motion from a central office? Local knowledge is often best served via channel partners who will probably be required for local billings and collections in many cases, and this may prove to be a more efficient option.

Most companies will look to their tax advisors, facilities teams, and operational teams to get this done. The real challenges are understanding the business benefit and building a clear vision for why a new office is the best course of action. If you are selling your new office proposal to your company, it will be vital to think through all the pros and cons and build a clear understanding of the hidden costs and challenges.

Here are a few examples:

1. **Hidden Costs of Ongoing Fiduciary Requirements and Compliance:** Expenses related to accounting and tax consulting alone could run into six figures each year. Because this money is likely to come from a different group's budget within your company, it may not be apparent, but this is a definite requirement for clarity and inclusion in the decision process.

2. **Hiring, Training, and Managing** a remote ecosystem comes with its own costs and challenges. Revisit the structure discussion in the previous chapter, will these people all report locally, or will they report to different managers in other locations due to their specific skills and departmental alignment?

3. **Setting Up International Locations:** Key considerations include who will be responsible for the office and the remoteness of the office. When planning how you will maintain your company's culture and ethical policies, consider if there is someone in the chain of command who will be able to protect the employees and the company's brand in case of inappropriate events or behavior.

   Putting an office in a foreign country may seem like an attractive project, coming as it may with the sheen of having a new international location. Just be sure to carefully weigh all the costs of running a remote team (money *and* time) against the benefits. You may find that keeping a team in a centralized hub and allowing for a little more travel is far more manageable. If you're unsure about the detail in making these decisions, I recommend investing in the advice of an industry expert, someone who can provide valuable context and point out the stumbling blocks.

4. **Delegate Carefully**: Finally, as your business grows, the easiest thing may be to delegate. However, allowing local managers or teams too much latitude in setting up entities or making decisions on people locations can create challenges down the road, as egos and short-term thinking can work against the bigger picture. Taxes are a good example of a risk you can avoid if you choose not to hire someone directly in a country where you do not have a legal entity. Take professional advice and think twice before agreeing to plans hastily prepared by regional staff who may have less experience or visibility into the total cost and your global strategy.

I had a manager in Spain who was desperate to hire a rep in Portugal, and she had the operating budget to do so. However, she did not realize the different legal frameworks and tax liabilities this would create, nor the cost of the required audit and fiduciary oversight. Despite the local need, her failure to understand the difficulty, risk, and true cost of managing a person in another country meant that delegating responsibility for a decision like this would have been a mistake.

Competencies and Role Types

In 2009, the Corporate Executive Board (acquired by Gartner) produced an excellent study that revealed five distinct profiles of sales professionals: *Hard Worker, Challenger, Relationship Builder, Lone Wolf,* and *Problem Solver.* While each profile proved unique and valuable, the Challenger was shown to be the most successful.

Understanding your customer and building a group of high performers who can acquire and manage them will require a laser focus on the *type* of individuals you hire. It is also important to consider your managers' strengths and weaknesses when vetting new hires. For instance, the Challenger will often appear abrasive and confrontational, and a leader who cannot embrace and motivate this kind of salesperson may not be cut out for high growth sales.

A leader in my charge was planning to terminate two salespeople because they were not "team players" and were disruptive and unwilling to participate and learn. But when I looked at the numbers, I found that these two individuals were among the highest performers on the team and had consistently delivered on their numbers, year over year. To be sure, disruptive people are not necessarily great for a team, but in this instance the *manager's* leadership and courage were lacking—not the salespeople—and when I offered these two a firm hand and strong guidance, they moved back into line and contributed strongly to the overall success of the business. Introverted and soft-hearted managers can struggle with strong salespeople. This does not make them poor managers, but they may be suited to roles where there are fewer Challengers or Lone Wolves to directly manage.

In the Gartner study, the other high performer was the Lone Wolf, an independent, self-assured individual who followed their own instincts and was apt to create division and hurt in the office. A familiar profile to most of us, the Lone Wolf was often such a high performer that they became unmanageable and acted with impunity. It is important to be able to discern between this individual and a Challenger, as managers who are not strong enough to manage the Lone Wolf personality risk losing other successful people who might not be able to tolerate the disruptions.

Problem Solvers, Hard Workers, and Relationship Builders all have a role to play as well, but success will depend more on where they sit and how they are managed. For example, the Relationship Builder's skills and disposition may be especially valuable in partner sales management, where helping partner companies sell with you is key, or in government sales, where service and relationship are more likely to be valued than a hard-hitting sales approach. Notably, the line to closed deals may be more circuitous or "dotted" with these three profiles than with Challengers and Lone Wolves.

There is real value in thinking through these role types as they apply to your team(s). Challengers and Lone Wolves may be the profiles that win the most attention and accolades, but depending on the size and

	Technical Sales	Principal Consultant	Technical Sales Manager	Inside Sales	Global Account Manager	Account Manager	Manager
Adaptability	✓	✓		✓	✓	✓	
Analytical Thinking	✓	✓			✓		
Building a Team and Collaborating			✓				
Business Acumen		✓	✓	✓	✓	✓	
Change Management			✓				✓
Collaboration and Team Leadership							✓
Commercial Drive and Initiative	✓	✓	✓				
Communication	✓	✓	✓	✓	✓	✓	
Communication for Managers							✓
Conflict Management					✓		✓
Cross-functional Focus			✓				
Customer Driven					✓	✓	
Customer Focus	✓	✓					
Decision Making			✓				✓
Diversity			✓				✓
Drives for Results				✓	✓	✓	
Emotional Intelligence			✓		✓	✓	✓
Influencing	✓	✓	✓				
Influencing and Negotiation				✓	✓	✓	
Innovative Thinking	✓	✓		✓			
Interpersonal Skills							✓
Leadership Performance and Action			✓				✓
Negotiating			✓				
People Development							✓
Performance Management							✓
Persuading							
Planning and Organizing		✓		✓	✓	✓	
Policies, Process, and Procedures				✓			
Problem Solving	✓				✓	✓	
Problem Solving and Conflict Management		✓					
Project Management	✓	✓					
Questioning or Curious	✓			✓		✓	
Strategic Agility			✓				
Strategic Management							✓
Teamwork and Collaboration	✓	✓		✓		✓	
Value Based Thinking					✓	✓	

FIGURE 3 Example Competency Matrix

structure of your sales organization, there are likely to be times when the unique skills and personalities of one of the other three profiles are exactly what are needed.

Competencies are another important factor in building the right sales force. I am constantly surprised by organizations that fail to build a set of competencies needed for each role type and then map this to their hiring process. Generally, between 30 and 40 competencies apply within Sales for different roles, and over the years these have evolved from simple terms like "negotiation" to more contemporary qualities like "emotional intelligence" and "curiosity." Around ten key competencies are normally prioritized for each role in a sales team. These are used to evaluate aptitude for the role during a new-hire interview process, in people development processes, and in considerations for promotion.

I recommend using the non-exhaustive list of competencies illustrated in Figure 3 when mapping to the roles in your sales organization.

Hiring

Close collaboration with your HR and talent teams is naturally prerequisite to great hiring. And when ramping a sales organization, involving HR in your annual planning cycles is key to successful execution.

For example, in a team of 300 growing at 20 percent, assuming a 15 percent annualized attrition rate, 75 people will need to be hired over the course of the year. In my experience with strong hiring functions, time-to-hire is normally around 45 to 60 days (excluding any notice periods required by a specific region or country), and it is critical to establish a clear methodology with your cross-functional team to get it right. For larger hiring campaigns, remember that the talent team will have to staff up to deliver on your requirements. This may take additional time and budgeting.

When interviewing, I recommend establishing a hiring panel for each role type, building a common set of questions and a process for the interviews (e.g., the STAR technique discussed below), and ensuring that each panel member understands their area of focus and how to document their findings. If panels get too large, they can devolve into bureaucracy and steal productive time from day jobs. I recommend a cross-functional panel of three or four, with one from the talent acquisition team as a professional recruiter who can ensure the process is well managed. When hiring more senior managers, a few more steps may be needed. For example, when running worldwide sales, I would insist on meeting every manager as a final interview to ensure the candidate's compatibility with the culture and values we were building. I cannot overstate how important this is; no matter how many people are under your purview, the first line is the most critical, and the way they represent you and relay your message will strongly impact your team's culture.

To quickly filter candidates, apply both the competency model and the STAR method, and for more technical and customer facing roles, don't be afraid to embrace presentations and other fun forms of interaction to test candidate skills. In my first startup we needed a delivery driver. We interviewed a store man I knew and liked who had come from a manufacturing industry I had worked in. My marketing manager, who was helping with the interview, said, "Well, if he's driving our cars, I better go on a ride with him to make sure he can drive!" Remember this practical approach, and if your prospective employee is going to give customer presentations and proof of concepts, take them for a "test drive" in a simulation of a customer session.

To be sure, during my years of hiring I got it wrong from time to time. In one situation where I allowed the hiring process panel to give me input, they recommended hiring a manager. My gut told me that the individual was not the right fit, but not wanting to rock the boat in my new role, I allowed the panel to sway me. While the candidate looked good on paper, he couldn't cope with the alpha pack of salespeople in his team, and we had to quickly replace him. This was most unfortunate, particularly for the poor manager who did his best and ended up having to go through a deeply challenging personal process.

Another time, during an internal audit, an individual was accused of certain irregularities. The company's process was world class, and our legal department conducted a thorough (and painful) review. Over the course of a few months, all the facts were gathered and analyzed, and the individual was eventually vindicated. During the process, I was asked how I had vetted and background checked the person in question. Fortunately, I had personally done the reference checks, calling a number of people the candidate had worked for to ascertain their credentials and quality.

In most large economies today, there are processes and companies that provide thorough background checks. Still, I encourage you to do your own and make sure your direct reports stand up to scrutiny. Not just the fiduciary checks but the relationships, teaming, and quality of work perspectives that can only come from a conversation with people who know and have worked with the candidate.

Having a record of the hiring process—of who asked specific competency questions, the candidate's answers, details of the candidate's perceived strengths and weaknesses, and each panel member's point of view—will be useful going forward as you see performance and churn within your team. This will also give you valuable insight into the accuracy of each panel member's assessments. It is not a scoring process per se, but it could help reveal who could be more helpful in future hiring, or where you could improve your process for selecting specific competencies for roles. I recommend staying very close to your talent acquisition team and constantly seeking feedback on how your sales managers are interacting and on their quality of hiring. I've found this to be a valuable early warning system for manager performance and business momentum.

After decades of both hiring and firing and getting it both right and wrong, if I had to give a one-word instruction, it would be *collaborate*. I've sat in a meeting where the hiring manager pointed the finger at HR when asked for a situation report for sales roles open for three months. HR in turn said they'd been waiting for availability of the hiring panel. This is unacceptable. Early on in my journey I began including hiring in weekly update meetings and looking at the numbers almost like a forecast. Ultimately, the hiring manager was on the hook for open heads in the system, and once this was clear and I called out hiring managers for it, the noise level dropped and collaboration massively increased. Remember, every open sales head is potential bookings lost: An unfilled sales rep position that carries a $3 million quota costs the company $250,000 in lost opportunity every month.

Using the STAR Method in Hiring

The STAR method (situation, task, action, result) was invented by a company called DDI in the 1970s, and it has proven to be one of the simplest and most effective ways to communicate in an interview. Whether you choose to implement the process through a professional service or embed it internally, it is particularly useful in establishing authenticity in the interview process. For example, you might ask an interviewee who claims they are experienced in change management to relate a specific situation where they used this skill. You might then ask for specifics around actions taken and results achieved, adding color to the assertion and helping you decide whether the individual's claim holds water.

Let's say you have identified the 12 competencies you are looking for in a new hire. You might staff a hiring panel with four members, and assign each panel member three of the competencies by which to assess the applicant. The panel would then convene at the end of the interview process to share notes, thus covering all competencies for the role and forming a more complete picture of the candidate.

Roles and Responsibilities

As companies grow or go through changes—like mergers, acquisitions, or restructuring—the clarity of roles and decision-making can suffer, causing the company to slow down due to confusing bureaucracy and politics. When risk is injected into a situation and it is unclear who is on the hook for a decision, no one is going to put their head up above the parapet and make that decision—it's just human nature. (Of course, the converse is true when things are going well and everyone wants to take a piece of that pie!) Resentment can build when the true architects of a win are not acknowledged, or when multiple departments are trying to do the same job, wasting time and duplicating effort.

To help create focus and clarify roles, I use two principles when designing my organizational structures. The first is MECE: All roles must be mutually exclusive and collectively exhaustive.[5] This means that clarity around global, regional, and local leadership, decision-making, account mapping, points of ownership on the sales motion, follow up, and communication should all be well documented, agreed, and followed carefully.

---

5   Developed in the 1960s by Barbara Minto at McKinsey and Company.

The second principle is RACI: responsible, accountable, consulted, and informed.[6] As businesses develop and matrices become established, clarity removes inertia and helps with faster execution. By way of example, consider Frank, my Swiss country manager, who was looking to hire a new SE manager. Because Frank was a direct report, the RACI process made him *responsible* for this hire. However, the EMEA or worldwide SE leader was *accountable* (or had to approve the hire), various departments needed to be *consulted*, and other team members needed to be *informed*. The RACI principle creates both clarity and a necessary synergy and tension between dotted-line and direct-line organizations, where one entity cannot act without the other in alignment. It also clearly maps responsibilities and decision ownership.

Management Playbook and Cadence

One of the most fundamental tools my teams and I have built over the years is a set of cadence documents and playbooks that clearly show the minimum expectation required for roles. We should never expect others within the organization to simply intuit or logic out what we are thinking and expecting. Rather, communication and clear expectation setting is foundational in creating a safe environment where teams know what it takes to get an A.

Figures 4 and 5 provide examples of real-life expectations that are simple and easy to communicate all the way to the field. Every company and every team will be different, but the theme will be the same, and thus the basic format of a quarterly cadence should be documented and regimented to bring clarity and alignment. When establishing

---

6   The RACI matrix was originally called linear responsibility charting (LRC), which was conceived by Ernst Hijams, a Dutch consultant, and later developed by a Canadian consulting firm Leethan, Simpson, Ltd in the 1950s.

yours, the key is to build a cascading system that supports the whole organization as a system within systems.

While I talk a lot about inspiration and strategy, the hard work of actual execution is where these playbooks reduce friction and where they really count. Repeatable processes, maniacal focus on the data, and consistent inspection are the hallmarks of great sales management. This is where the hard stuff lives, and unless you have established rigor and consistency, the team will feel it and will drift if they are not held to account.

A consulting friend of mine was coaching a chief revenue officer who continually seemed to be failing. The diagnosis in this situation was twofold. First, the CRO was more loyal than logical, so disciplining his people was hard (see section *Loyalty over Ability*). But he had also delegated the sales analysis and detail to his sales operations leader. While there were well-documented and succinct systems in place and the sales operations leader was world-class, the CRO had lost ownership and vital understanding of that detail and insight as well as a vital connection to his front-line sellers.

Imposing a cadence can be difficult, but I have found that when my teams workshop their own cadence, share best practices, and can see their "fingerprints" on the process, their buy-in is more assured. In Figures 4 and 5 I've shared some example cadence visuals for your team to use as templates.

PEOPLE	PASSION FOR OUR CUSTOMERS	PROCESS	PARTNERS	PIPELINE	PRODUCTS
• LEAD by EXAMPLE. • Clear MBOs (Management by Objectives). • Communicate clearly and often. • Clear career paths for all. • Positive (great) environment. • Skip level interaction where possible. • Community based activity and team building. • Coach often – curbside coaching and in-the-moment feedback • Invest time listening to your team.	• LEAD by EXAMPLE. • Plan to invest >50% of your time with customers and partners. • Be clear on what ACTIVITY is expected in each location you are responsible for. • Specific ACTIVITY-based targets for reps each week. • Track customer meetings, opportunity creation, and staff activity weekly.	• Focus on the KEY issues. • Interlock on common processes. • Avoid processes and communication that waste productive cycles. • Look for ways to interlock and be clear on your role and how you fit, avoiding duplication. • Challenge the system and work to make it better for all. • Strive to solve with systems and processes first, not simply more people. • Ensure there are documented plans for your business and clear milestones for success.	• Plan to Invest >50% of your time with customers and partners. • Track meetings, opportunity creation, and staff activity weekly. • Attend key QBRs and ensure clear meetings, alignment, outcomes and interlock are being driven. • VALUE the channel and look to scale and reach with the channel. • Listen and empathize: partners want to be heard and respected.	• CRM Hygiene is critical. • Clear visibility on your 12-month pipeline at all times. • Balanced Pipeline with your product suite. • Minimum 3x cover for your plan in quarter and next Q. • Close interlock with interdependent teams (like marketing) on your plans.	• Product enablement is a core part of your weekly cadence. • Drive weekly training and competitions with your teams. • Positive 2-way communication with the product group. • Be an expert in your technology and use cases. • Understand the competitive landscape and how you can WIN.

FIGURE 4 Being Race Fit: Your Gold Standard as a Sales Leader

ALWAYS	PLANNING	COMMUNICATION AND ALIGNMENT	ACTIVITY	PIPELINE
• Start your meeting with a crisp corporate message to ensure your strategy is clear and always the north star in your strategic meetings. • In channel meetings always start with a 5-minute high-level strategy and update. • Communicate often and never assume your audience understands. • Plan to invest as much time as possible face-to-face with customers and partners. • Aim for >110% of plan. Sprinters always aim to finish their race after the finish line. • Be mindful of your time and in what you are doing. Does it add to or dilute the goals you have set. • Know the ACTIVITIES that will drive the greatest outcome and work on these first.	• Clear documented plans for your accounts, territories, and partners. • Stored in a common location for all to use. • Accounts – In your CRM system of record • Channel – In a planned and well curated team repository. • Territories – In a planned and well curated team repository. • Clear action lists and activity plans. • Careful qualification of an in-or-out analysis – don't waste your time. • Ask for help and ask for reviews on your plans. Other people have great perspective and really do want to help you.	• Ensure you are aligned with your country and team strategy from accounts to channel and interlock between teams. • Ensure channel and sales are aligned on the same partners. • Think about your role and how you form part of the whole. • Team for >110%. How can you bring your team with you as winners? • Ask for help if you need it. We are in this together. • Communicate often and strive to lead by example. • Understand how your role interlocks with other teams – e.g., Marketing – and how you partner for success. • Seek to listen, to understand, and give people the benefit of the doubt.	• Understand the expected number of face-to-face meetings or calls per week that your manager believes are best practice for your role and for your location. • Clear measured ACTIVITY and outcomes. • Clear documented planning. • Fail to plan = plan to fail. • Document your activity in systems to measure success and what is working.	• Clear visibility on pipeline at ALL times. • Balanced pipeline with our product suite. • 3x cover for your plan in quarter and in next quarter (or more, aligned to your manager) • CRM system hygiene. • Align to corporate processes and support the use of systems so there are no private or bespoke repositories of information where information is not part of the global systems.

FIGURE 5 Being Race Fit: Your Gold Standard as an Individual Contributor

Setting Expectations

Aside from the basic job descriptions and roles of your managers and salespeople, setting clear expectations for your team as individual contributors or managers is key to achieving world-class performance, or a "gold standard" in excellence.

A good example of this was my Turkish team. Incredibly, they were getting more than ten face-to-face meetings a week with customers, and when I traveled to Istanbul—a sprawling city of over 950 square miles (2,500 square kilometers) with horrendous traffic—they were able to assemble at least half a dozen CISOs within hours, either for a group meeting or a meal. But I soon learned that this team's great benchmark was unrealistic for other teams, where customers perhaps liked longer sessions or were more difficult to meet with. Still, the example created positive tension, and I found that sharing it with my teams stimulated more activity. This is not due to any measurement I was doing; salespeople are just naturally competitive and want to improve.

In our offsites I eventually built the following basic slides as a regional leader and used them to discuss each team and establish a gold standard for performance.

Building a Quarterly Cadence Wheel by Week

The weekly cadence wheel is a simple tool that is easy to implement. It is a set of expectations that drives a predictable process for what will be required each week. Salespeople, including managers, are demotivated by surprises and spurious requests for information or meetings. Most understand the need for information and are very happy to collaborate, but providing a schedule ahead of time when something is needed smooths the process and improves morale. The weekly cadence wheel illustrated in Figure 6 is an example of an actual tool

I have used. Creating a tool like this normally requires a cascading set of priorities and schedules, from the board down, so that the process can be synchronized and information can flow up and down seamlessly when required.

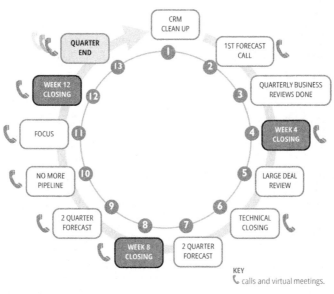

KEY
📞 calls and virtual meetings.

NOTES

WEEK 3   There will also be meetings at this stage, usually in smaller groups or different formats.

WEEK 5   There will also be a meeting at this stage, usually in smaller groups or different formats.

WEEK 6   Technical Sales team close their opportunities for the quarter.

WEEK 7   2 quarter forecast: a forecast for the current fiscal quarter and the next quarter.
          There will also be meetings at this stage, usually in smaller groups or different formats.

WEEK 9   2 quarter forecast: a forecast for the current fiscal quarter and the next quarter.

WEEK 10   Remove all pipelines from the quarter as they are unlikely to convert within the
          current quarter.

WEEK 11   Focus review on what is important for this quarter's success.

WEEK 12   As best practice, this week should always be treated like quarter end.

FIGURE 6 Example Week 13 Cadence Wheel

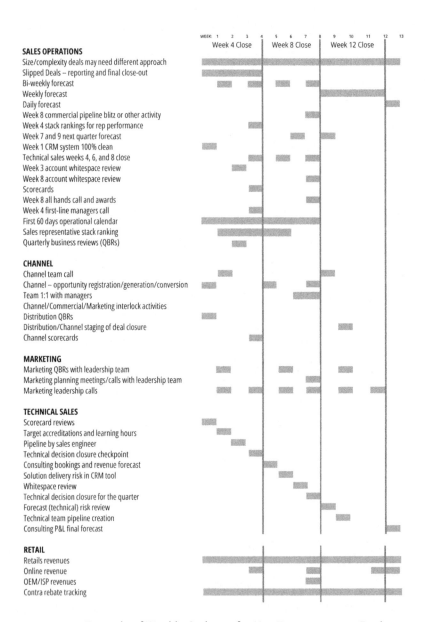

FIGURE 7 Example of Weekly Cadence for Key Events across a Region

Building a Quarterly Interdepartmental Calendar

The cadence wheel in Figure 6 would normally be the product of an interdepartmental sales calendar, one that takes into account different departments that work closely with sellers and other management activities that need to align to make salespeople more efficient, with as much of their time as possible assigned to customer-facing meetings or calls.

The calendar in Figure 7 illustrates a more detailed management cadence you might build to run a regional sales team, and while this example is quite complex, the organizational system and interlock is important whether you simplify or enhance it for your own organization.

This schedule is contingent upon global calendars and requirements and may need to be adjusted to coincide with feedback for board meetings or global leadership reporting. It is always best to start with the CEO and with board meeting schedules, and then cascade the rest of your department's subsequent initiatives and reporting into the CEO's high-level calendar.

Building a Management Playbook and Communication Strategy

Over the years, as I progressed up the leadership chain in the organizations I worked for, my ability to directly influence individual contributors became more and more diluted through the levels of management between me and the sales teams. I liken this to a lens or a filter, and like light that dims as it travels through a lens that is poorly focused or dusty, messages can be distorted as they move through the command structure, and the direction that your teams receive can be consequentially different from what you intended. I will discuss communication more in the *Art* chapter. Here I want to address the framework around which you can build a playbook, setting a standard for all managers within your organization to follow.

Ultimately, the clarity of your communication and your ability to consistently and successfully direct an organization will depend on a repeatable process. You must hire managers who are willing to collaborate, then enable them with a shared approach to industrializing your process, ensuring that the process is both worldwide *and* world-class. This way, when you send a message to the salespeople across all your global regions, it will read the same in Sydney, Boston, and Paris.

Building a playbook for a sales organization is reasonably simple for smaller organizations, and the section below, *Aligning to the 6 Ps*, will provide some guidance. On the other hand, building a playbook for a company that is already at scale or one that has been through acquisitions or mergers is a process that requires substantial collaboration and consultation to ensure that the whole management team buys in and sees the value.

While the process you build will be mandatory, it is pointless trying to enforce a system that doesn't work due to something you missed or something that needs revision because you failed to consult certain departments. "Measure twice and cut once," as nothing erodes trust and morale faster than the shifting floor of a brand new, mandatory set of rules that must then be changed because you didn't do your homework.

Each company is different, and your playbook will vary according to your company's size, geography, culture, product mix, existing processes, etc. But a practice I have found that adapts well is to build a high-level playbook with key pillars as a framework to hang enablement and a common structure around. I adapted a simple model called the 6 Ps as my reference, and then collaborated with my teams to build out frameworks that worked for them. The management playbook is slightly different from the product playbook or sales playbook as it mainly addresses the operating expectations and the management framework we will use to show exactly what excellence looks like.

An additional structural component I have built into several playbooks are the four pillars of People, Performance, Partners and Customers, and Data and Analytics. These pillars set out specific expectations upon which enablement teams and HR can build their processes and training so that everyone marches to the beat of the same drum.

1. People

    a. Talent and hiring
    b. Enablement
    c. Career development
    d. Recognition

2. Performance

    a. Planning
    b. Achieving a balanced scorecard
    c. Activity
    d. KPIs

3. Partners and Customers

    a. Expectations for the amount of customer face time required by the manager
    b. Expectations for personal attendance at business reviews
    c. Focus on customer retention and renewals and a close eye on this ecosystem
    d. Customer engagement, including CXO and multilevel engagement

4. Data and Analytics

    a. Cadence and expectations

    b. Process and hygiene

    c. The critical few activities that will make the biggest difference

    d. Alignment to the systems of record with no off-book systems being created

The Critical Few for Sales

Ultimately, you should distill the playbook, the weekly cadence, and the organizational construct down to a simple set of the critical few measures and focus activities that Sales will know are the most important—every day, every week, every month, and every quarter or year.

> Wallet cards are a helpful tool to put in play here. Every year, at our annual kickoff, we would create a set of cards with the "critical few" to highlight their importance and share a simple, common—and easily accessible—methodology for all to follow.

It is important to also develop an internal communications process with clear information on communication streams and where the latest information is coming from for the team to align to.

This is obviously a highly industrialized system designed for many hundreds, if not thousands, of employees, prompting the caveat that you should ensure you are implementing a process that is fit both for purpose and for the size of your organization. Start with the following section on the 6 Ps and decide how much process you and your business need for each item. These are important and will scale from small to multimillion-dollar companies.

Aligning to the 6 Ps

Some of our most successful years delivering growth (that did not come from one large deal or just one team) were built on simple principles our team could follow. A maniacal focus on winning was achieved by coming together as a team and asking ourselves what few things were the most important to execute on. As a result, we created our own version of the 6 Ps[7]: People, Pipeline, Partners, Products, Passion (for customers), and Process (see Figure 8). We figured that if we pulled together one or two specific KPIs for each of these areas, we would win. And we did—again and again—because it was a simple way to communicate a single strategy, from management all the way to the individual contributor.

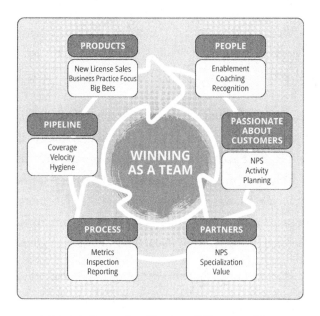

FIGURE 8 Example of Regional Plan on a Page

7   The 6 Ps of business is a marketing model developed by Neil Borden, a professor of marketing at Harvard Business School. The 6 Ps of selling is a sales methodology developed by Joe Girard. (Source: Google Bard)

Our one-page plan focused on:

- People
  - ▸ Enablement
  - ▸ Coaching
  - ▸ Recognition

- Pipeline
  - ▸ Coverage
  - ▸ Velocity
  - ▸ Hygiene

- Partners
  - ▸ NPS
  - ▸ Specialization
  - ▸ Value

- Products
  - ▸ New license sales
  - ▸ Line of business focus
  - ▸ Big bets

- Passion (for Customers)
  - ▸ Net Promoter Scores (NPS)
  - ▸ Activity
  - ▸ Planning

- Process
  - ▸ Metrics
  - ▸ Inspection
  - ▸ Reporting

Of course, setting priorities and focus areas is only half the job. Once we had quantified exactly what winning looked like for each of these measures, we then built a dashboard and reported on our progress as often as was reasonable. For some of the measures we could take a monthly snapshot, for many it was quarterly, and for others it was more nuanced. Some of the data was also not purely empirical, so for things like coaching or planning, for instance, we developed logical and realistic metrics.

I should also say that each team within my group did not necessarily follow the same dashboard. Figure 9 was my dashboard, but sales engineers, for example, had technical closure rates and customer health checks that were vital to customer Net Promoter Scores or velocity. The key in setting goals was to help managers and teams understand that it was not necessarily my measures that they needed to rigorously

SALES REGION X			COMMENTS	OWNER	FREQUENCY
PEOPLE	Employee Net Promoter Score (NPS)	⬆	Feedback sessions and numbers that drove collaboration	HR	Twice per year
	Attrition	⬅	Measure both voluntary and involuntary	HR	Quarterly
	Enablement	➡	Product enablement and process enablement	Enablement	Monthly
	Recognition	⬆	Measuring the number of awards by manager and dept	HR	Quarterly
PASSIONATE about CUSTOMERS	Customer NPS	⬅	If you don't have NPS, use renewal bookings info	Analytics	Quarterly
	Executive travel and customer face time	⬅	Measure exec engagement in customers. It counts!	Admin	Quarterly
PARTNERS	Partner NPS	⬅	Basic feedback loops are possible in the absence of proper NPS	Analytics	Quarterly
	New partners specialization	⬅	Normally your one area of focus to measure	SE Leader	Monthly
PRODUCTS	Product group A	⬅	Sales numbers easy to quantify	Ops	Monthly
	Product group B	⬆	Sales numbers easy to quantify	Ops	Monthly
	Partner group C	➡	Sales numbers easy to quantify	Ops	Monthly
PIPELINE	Coverage and velocity	➡	From CRM system	Ops	Monthly
	Usage and system hygiene	⬆	From CRM and planning, processes, and documentation	Ops	Monthly
	Customer whitespace and planning	➡	From planning and analytics	Ops	Monthly
PROCESS	Tools and process usage	➡	Overall use of systems and cadence	HR	Quarterly

FIGURE 9 High Level KPI dashboard

adhere to, but rather a critical few measures that unequivocally supported the goals and ultimately delivered to the board the outcomes they had requested.

Figure 9 is an example of the KPI dashboard from this high-level plan with each region having specific measurables behind each line item or an aggregation of measures consolidated into a line.

Setting Expectations for Role Types and Players

When setting expectations, I find it helpful to be as prescriptive as possible with the different roles within the teams, starting with robust discussions with each team about how many customers they meet with every week. In Istanbul, why could field sales achieve almost ten face-to-face meetings in a week while Germany was closer to five? There's no right answer—and thus no better team—but the discussions can be fruitful and help drive successful outcomes by setting achievable expectations by role.

A good example is new logo sales. If reps are not measured on a clear target number of cold calls you expected them to make to new logos, they will be unlikely to succeed. When baseline activities are not rigorously measured and clearly communicated, inertia has a way of overcoming creativity.

A great tool for driving the right behavior is gamification. Whether you achieve this through outright games or by introducing game-like goals to existing processes, the outcomes can be striking. In the Monday morning staff calls of one of my senior managers, each rep would be asked how many calls they had made, how much pipeline they had created, and how many deals they had closed in the prior week. Over time, as sales reps started feeling a sportsmanlike peer pressure within the group, it was amazing to see the size of the pipeline begin to correlate more directly with the number of calls made.

To make the "game" as fair and accurate as possible, we would measure the number of meetings held as a benchmark to determine if the rep was delivering enough activity. Our first-line managers would look for evidence that meetings had taken place in the minutes and notes to a customer thanking them for the meeting. This helped determine the true nature of the meeting and to separate the noise—let's face it, sales reps can sometimes "embellish" the truth when reporting on their activity—from the real work.

Balance vs. Bureaucracy

For leaders, particularly those who come from more regimented disciplines like finance, legal, or the military, it is a natural impulse to want to impose stricter measures when things go wrong. But when sales teams fail or results disappoint, the answer is not always to apply more rules.

I am constantly reminded that sales is 50 percent creativity and 50 percent systems and process, and if the creativity of sales reps is not nurtured, the exceptional will be lost in the mire of bureaucracy. One of the reasons I wrote this book was to highlight this delicate balance. While I embrace the many metrics and processes discussed here, I think they should be applied sparingly, intentionally, and thoughtfully.

There is almost an inverted logic here: While systems and processes are essential, freedom is what makes the magic happen in Sales. I liken this to field sports. Like most sports, soccer (football to my European friends) is governed by a set of rigorous rules that are actively (if not perfectly) refereed on the playing field. But once players take that field, they are free to use their reflexive athletic skill and split-second situational judgment to win the game. The point of all the rules and metrics—even down to the length and width of the pitch—is to give the players just the right amount of structure within which they can be their most creative.

I should add that the rules off the pitch count too. For the players, getting a place on the football team may be down to small things like showing up on time for practice, exercise regimes, and diet. In business, those "small things" might be completing a meeting report or updating a system—tasks that might feel repetitive or painful, but they may well earn you the right to "play on the field."

The best leaders understand this dynamic. They know that bureaucracy is just a "dirty word" for systems, process, rules, and enforcement, all of which are necessary, and they do their best to learn where to apply the rules and where they can loosen the reigns to let creativity blossom.

I have written a lot in this book about process, but if you remember only one thing, use it sparingly and only as much as necessary.

Inspection

Sales management and leadership are hard. Part of what makes them hard is how easy it can be to reach the wrong conclusions about the performance and outcomes of teams and individual contributors. This is down to, at least in part, the binary nature of sales results, which, if not properly analyzed, can make it very easy to form the wrong opinions.

Twenty years ago, I had a team leader in one of the countries I was managing. I really enjoyed working with him; he was always efficient and on time, he completed his sales reports, and when I visited, he always seemed exceptionally well prepared. He was a hard worker, conscientious, and a great relationship builder. So, I was shocked when my manager challenged me on his performance. Only when I looked at his growth against market, the number of leads he had converted, and how he compared with others in his group did I realize how badly he was performing. My loyalty and relationship with him had clouded my judgment.

Deep, objective inspection is vitally important. Unless you have the facts and understand your business, the assumptions you or your peers jump to may be difficult to dismiss—or confirm. I was attending a senior management meeting and we were struggling with the renewals sales of a certain product. Based on the numbers, the renewals team did not appear to be doing their job. But the manager had the details from his own inspection and had learned directly from his customers that a recent change in product strategy had resulted in the buyer deciding they no longer wanted the product. That meeting could have gone in a very different direction, but having the manager's inspection and direct customer intel enabled him to address the problem correctly, rather than just assuming that Sales had missed their number.

As you become more senior within organizations, the unfortunate truth is that assumptions can become perceived facts, and this can be very difficult to overcome. To counter this, you must learn to control the narrative by establishing fact before assumptions are made.

Partnering with HR, my operations director, and my finance director, we created a simple quarterly cadence, one that proved to be both highly manageable and transparent in building a clear inspection process. While keeping bureaucracy to a minimum, the simple process detailed in Figures 10 and 11 allowed for both quarterly measurement of every quota-carrying rep and feedback and advocacy from their managers. This ensured that extenuating circumstances or other facts were recorded and assimilated before actions were taken.

∨ WEEK 2

By the end of week 2 in the quarter, finance or operations should provide a performance report by the sales representative and by the manager for the prior quarter. Each first-line manager and HR business partner should be provided with their own specific report for their group. This report will include bookings attained and performance metrics against each individual's quota. Managers will also have information about the number and percentage of their reports who are on target.

∨ WEEK 3

First-line managers then have week 3 to consider action by sales representatives, which can include coaching, improvement plans, or other tools. HR should meet with each first-line manager and agree, by sales representative, on the specific action to be taken, and then document it.

∨ WEEK 4

Regional leaders meet with their sales managers and HR and analyze every sales representative's performance and agree/finalize plans. An estimated 5% of sales representatives will end up on some kind of plan at any given point in time. Sales managers' performance should be based on their sales representative's success rates, and usually a sales manager with less than 60% of their staff being above 80% of quota should be on some form of the improvement plan as well.

∨ WEEK 5

Regional leaders along with HR meet with senior sales / global leadership, present the aggregated plans, and advocate for their team and receive signoff from senior management that the correct plans are in place to appropriately manage performance for the previous quarter.

FIGURE 10 Sales Representative and Manager
Quarterly Performance Process

While it is true that freedom makes the magic happen in Sales, sales teams nonetheless thrive on structure and on knowing the rules. It's a kind of freedom paradox in Sales. Surprises and changes in expectations can create dissent and uncertainty, which can affect morale, proactivity, and ultimately, productivity. Whatever metrics or process

2 Quarters ago (completed the previous quarterly)

Name	Role	Target	Actual	% Achieved		Manager Success		Action
Sally	Manager	800	870	109%	✓	3 of 8 reps	✗	*verbal discussion and coaching of sales representatives with plan below 60%
Bill	Individual	100	500	500%	✓			Recognition for large deal
Anne	Individual	100	50	50%	✗			No action – new hire
Farid	Individual	100	50	50%	✗			No action – large deal and pipeline imminent
Mike	Individual	100	50	50%	✗			Coaching
June	Individual	100	50	50%	✗			Personal improvement plan
Fred	Individual	100	40	40%	✗			Personal improvement plan
Jolene	Individual	100	70	70%	✓			No action required
Joel	Individual	100	60	60%	✓			No action required

Last Quarter (being completed in current quarter per the process outlined above quarterly)

Name	Role	Target	Actual	% Achieved		Manager Success		Action
Sally	Manager	800	610	76%	✓	6 of 8 reps	✓	*No action because she is measured on the # of sales representatives succeeding
Bill	Individual	100	100	100%	✓			N/A
Anne	Individual	100	120	120%	✓			N/A
Farid	Individual	100	50	50%	✗			2nd Q – move to an improvement plan
Mike	Individual	100	80	80%	✓			Great progress on coaching plan
June	Individual	100	70	70%	✓			Great progress on coaching plan
Fred	Individual	100	40	40%	✗			Move to formal process or exit
Jolene	Individual	100	80	80%	✓			N/A
Joel	Individual	100	70	70%	✓			No action required

*Naturally, at year-end, if Sally is below plan, this becomes a different discussion, but during the journey, there is a balance between overall performance and the percentage of her sales representatives making plans. A great leader does not survive on just one or two people making their number.

FIGURE 11 Example Performance Report

you may use, make it simple, uncomplicated, and logical, and your team will align, be energized, and feel "free" to deliver incredible outcomes.

As the process for inspection builds, quarter on quarter, you should see the most well-liked reps being given air cover by their managers, but because the snapshots are recorded and reviewed in retrospect, it can become extremely difficult to find shade where performance can be reviewed over several quarters in one meeting. Data is key here and the "science" needs to be solid so that emotion can be taken out of decision-making and the company can benefit from logical, defendable, and relatively fast decisions.

QBRs (Quarterly Business Reviews)

Not all quarterly business reviews should be internal. Some of the most successful salespeople I have worked with conduct QBRs with their largest clients, thereby creating a platform for the most senior people in both organizations to gather, align, and create value. I came to call these quarterly *value* reviews and sought to establish milestones with the customer around "past value delivered."[8]

Of course, QBRs—both internal and with clients—are not only for reporting and data analytics; they are an opportunity to align, build loyalty, establish and grow relationships, and assure team members in the field that they are part of something bigger. Energy, focus, and alignment are some of the key outputs from a great QBR.

Format and Cadence

In Dubai, where I lived and worked for 15 years running globally disparate teams, even in the 1990s and early 2000s the cost of gathering every quarter was prohibitive. This was a time when video conferencing was far from common and we had to work hard at virtual meetings, which only worked if the format was right and if the overall cadence included face-to-face meetings. When Covid finally stopped travel, I found that my normal internal business process didn't change that much, but it did give me a head start in understanding that the world was changing to a more virtual operating experience. My one caution is that while

---

8   Thank you, Steve Thompson, for drilling this into me over many years!

virtual can be a cost effective and strategic tool, I have found over the years that face-to-face is an absolute necessity. If you are an individual or a very small group, I recommend meeting monthly at a minimum. Once your team grows to 25 or more, bringing team leaders together a minimum of every six months for face-to-face meetings is key for alignment, mental health, and a sense of connection to the company strategy.

In my experience, when face-to-face QBRs were more than five months apart, sales leaders from different countries or regions would begin to feel disconnected and issues would begin to arise. The cadence of face-to-face every six months, while easy to fit into a calendar, was not necessarily optimal, and I would try to make sure that we met more frequently. For software companies with an annual budget cycle, the cadence for face-to-face meetings would begin with the Q1 global sales conference, where I would always program management side meetings or even full management training days. The Q2 QBR would then be virtual, with optional personal visits to underperforming regions. Q3 QBR would be face-to-face if possible, and I would normally run a half-year "reset" alongside my QBR where I invited extended managers to look at performance, understand needed soft changes, and begin an early outlook for the next fiscal year around needed changes and improvements. By Q4, leaders would begin to feel the fatigue of their nine-month sprint, and by the middle or end of the first month of the quarter, a physical meeting of just the senior leaders for a QBR was a chance to sense-check the annual plan, prepare for the following year, and, most importantly, ensure alignment in hearts and minds. Additionally, my QBRs always devoted at least half a day to a CSR (corporate social responsibility, or "giving back") event, and to some sort of team-building activity. (I will cover this more in the *Art* chapter.)

Most QBRs I ran were three-day events, with two days of data and meetings followed by a day for team building and CSR. From a programming perspective, one of the most frustrating formats I have encountered is what many know as "death by PowerPoint." Having someone travel by plane and stay in an expensive hotel room just to recite the text on a slide is massively wasteful. I insisted that presentations be provided 48 hours before meetings and that *all* presentations be reviewed and understood well before the meetings began. In a 45-minute session, I asked leaders to spend 20 minutes on what they thought were the salient points and devote the rest of the time to discussion and debate.

Companies live and die by the teams they create, and in Sales QBRs it is vitally important to include intradepartmental teams. This may include Finance, HR, PR, Marketing, Operations, Channel, Sales Engineering, and anyone else closely associated with successful customer outcomes. A good example of this kind of inclusive collaboration was one QBR where we discussed an expected 50 percent growth number and projected hiring for the coming year. The support of HR and talent through our growth phase was critical, and if they had not been in the room and at the inception of that plan, the likelihood of failure would have increased. No one likes to be handed a task with no strategic context for that task. Being involved in the "why" and in the fundamental building of a plan brings alignment on both purpose and outcome.

Finally, as the leader of the group it is hugely important to provide key business data and your synopsis of the business. After pleasantries and expectations setting, I always opened my meetings by diving into the synopsis, as both a level setting and scene setting exercise. This ensured that our focus was on the right outcomes for the duration of the meeting. Equally important are operational leadership and the support of a strong operational business partner who provides insight and recommendations, more than just a pack (a financial and operational summary of the current state of the business). If you get this part of your QBR right, and your data is up to scratch, in the first 60 minutes, you can change the outcome of your three-day meeting and possibly your entire quarter.

Root Cause Analysis

How many of you have heard the rant "just get it done!" from your manager? The manager's temptation to blunt-force their way past conditions and complexity are all too human, but the gap between this exhortation and actually "getting it done" can often be quite difficult to navigate, especially when issues and obstacles are poorly (or wrongly) understood. Sometimes the job of the leader is to change a team's perception of reality, that is, to correct the record on what an issue actually is or what it means. At other times, the root cause of a given issue may be elusive, obscure, or simply unknown. In every case, the path to success will be clearer when the leader addresses obstacles with empathy, coaching, and methodology.

My tool of choice for diagnosing and addressing root cause has been the cause-and-effect fishbone diagram invented by Kaoru Ishikawa. This tool is helpful in uncovering the potential causes of specific events or issues and allowing for further analysis of each perceived cause. Understanding cause and effect in a more objective and non-confrontational way with teams can be powerful and productive as it alleviates blame while allowing the business to focus on the root causes of points of failure. I have found that even when a team may bear some responsibility for problems, using a logical and objective tool like Ishikawa's fishbone diagram can make it easier to move past blame and get to solutions.

For example, let's say the renewal rates are dropping for a product line. This may be due to any number of underlying factors that have not been clearly communicated. A root cause analysis in a situation like this can potentially uncover "low hanging fruit" issues like, say, a poor billing experience or an easily remedied customer service access problem. Where the temptation may have been to address a shortfall with a price incentive, now you have an opportunity to preserve your margin while increasing customer satisfaction.

> This may seem basic, but the number of times in organizations where I have seen a refusal to accept the facts due to politics or stubbornness compels me to recommend a process. Write it down, and make it plain. Workshop across functions and remove the personalities, and the logic will shine through.

A good root cause analysis looks at problems like layers of an onion, and I have found that addressable issues are usually at least six layers deep. Once you do identify a root cause, you can begin plotting a way forward, and I have found that RACI is particularly useful here. I also recommend keeping three foundational elements of your business in mind when planning: your shareholders, your employees, and your customers. Keeping these stakeholders in mind will help you build cohesive, winning plans.

Failure, Gap Plans, and Performance Management

Failure is not always someone else's fault. There will be many occasions where you or your team fail, and you will have to own it and deal with it. Just know that boards generally prefer straight talk, not excuses. They want clear-eyed explanations of what happened and the options for fixing a situation or doing better next time. As a leader, leaning into this and being the first to put your hand up and be proactive is almost always the right approach.

One quarter we failed dismally, and it happened in the very last week. There were mitigating circumstances, of course, but instead of finding excuses, I worked with my team all weekend aggregating the root causes, looking at what we could do better and what we could do differently. We covered people, process, technology, our partner ecosystem, training, staff changes, personal improvement plans, and our execution timeline. The document I sent through Monday morning was thorough, beginning with an executive summary for easy consumption and a clear SMART (specific, measurable, achievable, realistic, timebound) plan of action we would deliver on in the coming month to course correct and, more importantly, to give confidence to executive management and the board that we had clear command and control. This resulted in complete trust from the board and zero knee-jerk or micromanagement. Through candor, diligence, and a little bravery, we controlled the narrative, and in the process we gave our leaders the tools *they* needed to manage up and provide context and confidence.

When things are not working, you must own the narrative and communicate clearly and *promptly*. Being frank and direct is key, and "speaking truth to power" (a rule I learned early on) definitely applies here. This can be tough, but if you control the context, the preparation, and the narrative, especially with a strong team and air cover from your manager, you can execute well through crises.

It is important to speak briefly about the "truth" part of speaking truth to power. There is a danger in that your truth may be more about your perceptions than facts, and you must guard against making assertions that may not hold up under objective or logical scrutiny. I have made this mistake in the past and it has cost me dearly. You may be tempted, for example, to blame the quality of a product when there is a deeper problem on your team that you're trying to avoid or deflect attention from. Getting to the root cause is vital, and making sure that you do not adopt the position of your peers for the sake of convenience can be difficult but is nevertheless the mark of true courage and leadership. Speak truth to power and ensure that it is rooted in your own research, that it is defendable, fair, logical, and goes directly to a solution. If you raise a problem (or have created one), always try to bring a solution.

Performance Improvement Plans

When I was a regional director, I grew deeply frustrated with a particular individual and really wanted to fire him. Over time, I had recorded the challenges with him and accumulated enough documentation to give HR the latitude they needed to help, but my vice president, in his wisdom, stopped me. A former professional footballer, he told me a story about the power of coaching one of his players through a rough patch to a successful outcome. I swallowed hard and began a journey with this individual where we sat down twice a week, an hour at a time, with a painful, line-by-line action plan comprising tasks, outcomes, dates, and progress on every single thing that needed to be done or improved on.

After a month, we began meeting once a week. The meetings were often contentious, gritty, and raw, but progress, slow at first, began to improve. Month two arrived and it became apparent that this individual had crossed a threshold and was delivering results that were twice what I expected. The meetings ended, he moved on to solo flight, became one of my very best performers, and he is now a close and lifelong friend.

My VP was right and I was wrong, but I chose to swallow my pride and invest in genuinely drawing alongside someone I had wanted to terminate. As a result, we not only changed the outcome but I gained a friend and won the respect of my team, who clearly witnessed the process.

Not all improvement plans have fairy-tale endings, and some performance management will, of necessity, be fast and surgical. Just be sure to ask for advice, especially when someone's livelihood is at stake. Unfortunately, and particularly in the U.S., many employers see performance improvement plans as a tool to reduce risk and facilitate termination. To build trust, I encourage you to think differently, commit to the process, and show your team that it is called a "performance improvement plan" for a *good* reason.

Decisions Are Your Legacy

I have seen both great and terrible decisions made during my career, from nepotism to choosing an office space because it is close to someone's house to strategic decisions that have helped underprivileged children receive technology that bridges the digital divide. When you are in a position of power, you have the opportunity to make decisions that impact not only you and your team, but also the world around you, leaving a legacy that is much greater than the sum of its parts.

In most companies there are three core stakeholder groups you should carefully consider when making decisions in a for-profit environment: (in no particular order) your customers, your employees, and your shareholders. Strive to make decisions that equally benefit or equally challenge all three of these groups.

Logic should be at the heart of decision-making, and even (or especially) when you may be inclined to go with your gut on a decision, going through a logical process of scenarios and outcomes with a partner on a whiteboard to challenge your thinking is a brilliant way to avoid missteps. My process normally involves information gathering for a specific issue, which may include a root cause analysis and data around best practices. Often, I will consult the internet for some of these best practices if there is no local knowledge, and then parse this information with my team and colleagues.

At the end of the day, your decision should be defendable by sound logic that gives you the confidence to stand up and own it. This may not make you the most popular person, but you'll earn respect—and you must accept that you will never please everyone.

> Even leaders I have not liked have won my respect over time through their record of great and fair decisions. Ultimately, I want to be remembered for building a great legacy and reputation, and this comes down in part to the decisions I make every day.

Deal and Account Reviews

One of the most basic cadence actions I drove as a senior sales leader was running regular account reviews. Friday afternoons were a great time to look at two or three account plans or deal reviews with some of the sales reps to really understand what they were working on. We selected the accounts based on large deals potentially happening in the following quarters or on strategic accounts we were trying to develop. We kept away from deals in the current quarter as I wanted to separate strategy and planning from tactical forecast calls. These review calls resulted in both a deeper understanding of the customer environment and much closer alignment and tighter relationships with some of our top salespeople. Some of these relationships have endured for decades.

The account review templates we used varied from company to company. We looked at each customer strategically, considering our technology, their needs, the white space, the competition, and our ultimate objectives. Some of the best reviews included org charts, aspects of Power Base Selling (Holden International), Challenger selling (Challenger Performance Optimization, Inc.), and Target Account Selling. The challenge was to keep it simple enough to use but detailed enough to align to the potential deal size. The same approach applied to channel-based plans and territory plans.

Within actual deal reviews I always looked for the rep's strategic approach to providing overviews and detailing customer needs, and I used different tools depending on the sales and account planning methodologies used by the team. I tried not to apply too much bureaucracy in terms of format and specifics—some reps used PowerPoint while others preferred Excel—as what mattered more were a set of data points, a critical understanding of the account, and the objectives and the actions required and measured to achieve a great outcome.

As the reviews began to move into actual deals, I tended to use the MEDDPICC[9] process wherever I could, and I found that giving my sellers clear expectations of the questions I would ask dramatically reduced fear and uncertainty about the reviews. Leaders often ask questions that they know staff members don't have answers for, but the purpose of these reviews was not to look smart or get "one over" on an unsuspecting salesperson. I wanted to convey to the team that while I may have been the senior sales leader, I was still part of the team that could help drive a deal, and in that context, the seller was on point and I was part of *their* team. Cultivating a trusted relationship where deal strategy and planning could be safely debated gave energy, focus, and momentum to our salespeople. It also gave me insight, and I was able to constructively provide help, input, and wisdom without bureaucracy.

---

9   Metrics, Economic Buyer, Decision Criteria, Decision Process, Paper Process, Implications of Pain, Champion, and Competition. Originally designed in PTC as MEDDIC and trademarked by Jack Napoli.

Figure 12 illustrates the kind of MEDDPICC questions I would ask. Note that I have kept the questions extremely simple to avoid fear and build trust with the team.

M Metrics

What outcomes do they want to achieve and by when?
How will they measure success (metrics)?

E Economic Buyer

Who will make the economic decision (individual or committee)?
Who cares about the outcomes and influences that individual or committee?

D Decision Process

What/who are the buying steps, timeline, and owner of each step?

D Decision Criteria

What are the decision criteria and do they support the desired outcomes?
Did we influence them or are we responding to someone else's criteria?

P Paper Process

What is the customer's preferred contract format and signing process?

I Identify Pain

What business problem or opportunity are we helping the customer address?
What is our value proposition so they will want to choose us now?

C Competition

What alternative are we competing against (Competition, Do Nothing, or Do It Themselves)?
What is our strategy for winning?

C Champion

Who is our Champion?
Why are they our Champion and how do you know?

FIGURE 12 Qualify the Opportunity

MEDPICC Example with Key Questions

Developed from the original work done by Dick Dunkel
and John McMahon while at PTC

Leading and Lagging Indicators

As my team's sophistication grew in the mid-2000s, our approach to measuring success and outcomes also changed. Simple levers and data points around quota and direct extrapolation of quota attainment were great for flagging areas of concern, but they did not change the destination of our ship, and often that ship was too close to shore before we could change the facts. The bottom line was that the quarter-end results that were obvious to everyone were not going to change our course *during* the quarter. We needed metrics that could show us where we were *going*, not where we had been, and in time to course correct before we grounded the ship.

A good example of this is telling your team to make more new logo sales, and possibly even changing the comp plan to create some incentive. You may achieve limited success with this approach, but likely with no more than 20 percent of the team. Building success within the *whole team*, on the other hand, takes a more fundamental change in behavior and may come down to driving basic activities. In the case of new logo sales, that might be tracking the number of new logo calls or rewriting call scripts. Changing the measurement of activity here, instead of the compensation plan, would be more effective.

As we developed our cadence and became more adept at enterprise selling, a number of leading and lagging indicators emerged. Figure 13 shows some examples we used at a specific point in our journey.

I should note here that too many data points can be worse than no data points as information overload can stifle a team. But this is a carefully vetted list that evolved organically in a real-world enterprise selling environment, one that might serve as a helpful starting point or template to help you build your own critical few items that need focus and the leading indicators of success and basic levers you need to make them happen.

LEADING INDICATORS	LAGGING INDICATORS
• People – hiring and attrition	• Sales representatives
• Skip level reviews	Participation rates
• Regional surveys	• Manager's team participation
• Pipeline coverage	rates
• Pipeline velocity	• Analysis by deal size, number
• CRM hygiene	of deals, velocity, product
• Average deal size	• Bookings and velocity
• Account plans	• Forecast accuracy and
• Quarterly business reviews –	linearity
internal and external	• Solutions and product mix
• Services book of deals	• Loss reviews
• Balanced pipeline	• Feedback
• Forecast detail and depth	○ Customer
• Deal resourcing and depth	○ Partner
• Bridge and improvement plans	○ Competitor
• Marketing activities	○ Journalist/Press
• Technical capability and	○ Analyst
leadership	
• Channel health	

FIGURE 13 Example of Leading and Lagging Indicators

Developing First-Line Managers

In 2009, when I was promoted to vice president at Symantec, I immediately confronted a new reality. I needed to get a sales team of hundreds of sellers in multiple countries to come together and drive the business to new heights. I needed them to not only be great, but to be the very best. In spite of that, my first quarter was an absolute disaster, and I came to realize that I couldn't do it all on my own. I had to do more than lead, I had to learn to *inspire*, and as my key leadership team came together, I realized that I also needed to double down on enablement, particularly for our first-line managers.

> The more time I spend in leadership, the more I realize how important it is to build a great first-line management culture and process. Part of my hypothesis is that if you have a poor sales rep but a great first-line manager, the rep will likely be replaced quickly, and the manager will cover any gaps. On the other hand, if you have a bad first-line manager, not only will their great salespeople leave but the manager will fail to close any deals when they experience the inevitable attrition.

My first step in building an enablement process was to build a cadence into my quarterly plan where I ran book clubs[10] and delivered manager-specific, quarterly, all-hands calls that were hard hitting and shared the unvarnished facts, all with the intent of bringing the team "into the room." This resulted in overwhelming support and commitment to our shared challenges.

Naturally, the work of product training, sales pitches, and competency mapping are all massively important parts of enablement, but this is "all in a day's work" for most enablement leaders. As a leader, learning to inspire and focusing on the managers are key pieces that are often overlooked.

The next step in this journey was developing our leadership pipeline. We realized that unless we needed skills, experience, or insight from outside our company, the best way to grow our management team was by promoting from within. As we began to give our best and brightest the opportunity to grow, it unlocked the whole team's sense of career

---

10 In these book clubs I would choose a book, based on our current situation and learning needs, and give it to all my managers for the quarter to read. We would then review it the following quarter. I selected high performers to help me present it, and the process resulted in lots of constructive discussion and feedback.

opportunity, growth, and energy, and the business flourished. This was a powerful motivator, and although it may be hard for smaller organizations, as you reach critical mass and need to scale, retaining, developing, and promoting embedded talent will be a key strategic imperative.

No doubt, many of you in management positions have received emails from HQ asking for a list of your key people before salary increase time. And you've probably been frustrated by the tactical nature of this work, which is normally designed to deliver against a specific event or requirement and is then filed away. A better approach is an end-to-end process that encapsulates annual reviews, performance, potential, and enablement in one virtuous cycle that dynamically evolves to meet the needs of your best and brightest. We found that building a system like this in our first-line manager programs enabled us to use this data and system for everything from annual reviews to performance management to promotions.

Of course, HR was a key stakeholder in all of this, and partnering with them enabled us to take advantage of their understanding of the process of employee development and maintaining this cycle. Over time we developed a clear list of individual contributors, managers, and executives who were put into development programs and projects to enhance their readiness for bigger roles as well as plans to retain them through involvement in interesting work that showcased their value.

I have been extremely fortunate in my career to have managers who included me in many such programs—from participating in staff development to vertical markets leadership to global go-to-market planning and collaborating with global consulting firms to sitting on global ethics and compliance committees. I embraced all these opportunities as they made me better and encouraged me to buy into the company, intellectually. For all those leaders who have made an impact in my life (and you know who you are), you have my most sincere thanks.

Pipeline Generation

Pipeline generation can take many forms, but whatever form it takes, one thing is certain: What gets measured gets done.

In addition to the pipeline you expect to see generated organically, consider the best practice of organizing what we called "pipeline generation days," where we'd gamify the process and bring the entire region together to focus on a single set of objectives like a product, a vertical, or a specific outcome. During these get-togethers, simple activities, like competitions between teams and countries around various measurable datapoints, made for exciting days with great prizes for the teams and members who made the biggest difference.

As with all things, however, there can be downsides to measuring the wrong things. For example, measuring pipeline created in financial terms might encourage sales reps to hide deals for the weeks preceding pipeline day, or prize-hungry reps may create a huge amount of over-inflated deals or fake pipeline. Instead, consider rewarding activities like the number of partners involved in your pipeline generation day, the number of people a rep may train as subject matter experts, the number of calls made, or the number of follow-up appointments achieved. These are much more basic measures and are more aligned to leading indicators.

Remember, the results you post publicly and the metrics you reward your team on can differ greatly from what you analyze internally with the more senior people in your organization. As you drive your pipeline generation days, your operations teams should be analyzing the impact on the pipeline over the following month. This should give you more "telemetry" and help reveal which activities drive the greatest pipeline. Just be careful what you show your team, as they will all be watching you to understand how they can win your approval or move forward in the organization. Dollars in the pipe and particularly building fake, overinflated pipeline are real challenges because these metrics affect the company's financial forecast, hiring strategies, and the operational decisions you make for your business. We all want to believe great news when we receive it, but ensuring that your data is realistic by helping your people focus on the metrics that will build genuine deals and dollars will ultimately deliver the right behavior and affect the quality of your pipeline.

The paragraph above required years of experience to write, and I hope that you can learn from my journey and avoid unnecessary pain in yours. Pipeline generation and real qualification are hard, and the last thing you need is to obfuscate the facts through overinflated numbers from reps who are trying to win short-term accolades.

CHAPTER THREE

The Art

This chapter of the book may follow *Science*, but in selling I have come to see *art* as equal in importance, forming half of a truly successful—or whole—sales story. While short-term sales can be gained through clinical assertion of science, true creativity and culture are built on more than just numbers. This chapter follows *Science* simply because even a great sales culture is for nothing if it is not making money.

One of the most interesting things about Sales is that it requires creativity and passion to really shine. Over the years, I have begun my leadership journey with many sales teams with a recap of Maslow's hierarchy of needs because the concepts are so profound. For example, if (heaven forbid) you were drowning, the only thing on your mind would be getting to dry ground, and your desire to survive would supersede your need to know if your purse or cell phone were safe. The hierarchy of needs brilliantly illustrates how each step up a level requires the level we are on to be under control.

It is no surprise then that safety and personal security are one level up from physiological needs. Mapped to our work life, this means job and career safety (see Figure 14). Thus, sales leaders who build cultures where teams can not only survive but thrive are, in an important way, creating safety for their salespeople to reach their fullest potential. I cannot overemphasize this. If instead your style were to lay down the law, instill fear, and rule with an iron fist, your people would never feel secure, and while they may perform adequately, they would always be spending valuable energy and time on their own safety. They would be unable to reach that point of transformation described in the work of Richard Barrett[11], where team members move from being unsure, or "half in and half out," to being fully committed, putting their hearts and their passion into the work and the people they work with.

11 For more on Richard Barrett's model, see www.valuescentre.com/barrett-model

Self-Actualization	Creativity. Acceptance, **Purpose.** What I do is for the greater good. I set an example and motivate others. The sky is the limit.			**HIGHLY ENGAGED**
Self-Esteem	**Confidence.** Achievement, Importance. I am a vital part of the business. I make a difference. I make things happen.			**ENGAGED**
Belonging	**Sense of Connection.** I know I am part of something bigger. I am proud to work here with a team. I am still holding back a little.			**ALMOST ENGAGED**
Security	**Employment.** If I don't feel secure, I will probably retreat and do the least I can. I'm here for the money, even if I don't like it.			**NOT ENGAGED**
Physiological Needs	**Survival.** My work does not excite me. I don't want to be here.			**DISENGAGED**

Each layer is foundational to your potential in the next level.

FIGURE 14 Maslow's Hierarchy Applied to Engagement Impacting Potential

When salespeople are allowed and enabled to operate at the top of the pyramid, fully self-actualized and with appropriate creative freedom, they will be able to make the best—and most complex—deals happen. Every action and every decision you make as a leader should take this into account as you build a culture that enables your people to achieve a sense of security, belonging, and self-esteem. The further up the pyramid you are able to climb in this effort, the more upsides for you and your team, both in the numbers and in personal fulfillment, not to mention enduring relationships.

This is part of what I call the "art" in leadership and management, and in this chapter of the book, I will explore other ways I have built art into my style and my process.

Finding Balance

If you are a new CRO or sales leader, a new revenue target will likely weigh heavily on you while you are considering how to execute and drive your team. And especially if you were recently promoted, the added urge to do your subordinates' jobs for them, or simply do too much, can create a tinderbox of tension that can easily ignite into negative emotions, frustration, or confrontation.

Finding balance, where you can bring your team along on your journey while driving for results, is a narrow needle to thread, and great sales leaders build strong legacies by tapping into strong EQ skills while maintaining their integrity and commitments.

> The president of a company I worked for some years ago told me I could always regain bookings through new deals or turn around lost deals, but my brand and my trust, once broken, were potentially irreparable.

I have always approached my team with the perspective that I am there to serve *them*. There is no room for arrogance or subservience in real leadership. Listening and showing respect and appreciation are marks of the kind of leadership that engenders loyalty and inspires follower-ship. We will explore balance more in the sections ahead.

The Basics

If the word "basics" feels a little reductive or, well, *basic*, for this book, nothing could be further from the truth! While you will know these terms well, my goal here is simply to reinforce how important it is to think very carefully about them. After all, what you *intend* can often be different from how your intentions are *interpreted* or perceived. Staying grounded in these principles is no guarantee that everyone will be "singing from the same song sheet," but they can serve as helpful reminders of the kinds of things we can sometimes neglect or forget, perhaps precisely because they're so very basic.

- **Trust** is a bedrock requirement of all good leadership.
- Your team must believe you when you make commitments, so **honesty** is key when communicating.
- You can bring **candor** to your messages without being abrupt or confrontational.
- Be sure to examine what type of a person you are; **self-awareness** is essential to communicating authentically.
- Regardless of your personal style—direct, casual, business-like, personable—always communicate with **empathy**.
- Be careful not to soft-sell or muddle the truth when **clarity** and candor are called for.
- Above all, **authenticity** is key to successful leadership. Once lost, it is very hard to regain trust.

Attitude Affects Altitude

When I was a junior manager and I traveled to our regional HQ, I was often one of the first in the office in the morning, and I would set up at a hot desk in the open plan area, just outside the bank of executive offices. When the SVP arrived, I would watch and wait for the briefest of nods or a simple smile of acknowledgement. These small gestures would always energize me, and that's why, as a leader, I have tried to be ever mindful of the people around me, encouraging, listening, and acknowledging.

Spending an extra 15 minutes on the way to and from a meeting to simply connect with people can make an incredible difference. Showing up with a positive mindset, leading with a smile, and being proactive are infectious behaviors that cost you nothing. Authenticity is vital, of course, and if things are not great, there is no use in pretending. But in both good and challenging times, attitude affects altitude in yourself and in those around you, and this is especially true if you are a senior leader.

First, Be a Giver

If you are starting in a new company or have just been promoted into a new role, as a new leader it is vital that you step up and set the tone. If you want your team to trust you, you must give trust first, and if you want your team to feel safe, you must provide safety in the form of air cover and clarity.

> Whenever I began a new role or started in a new company, I always built a presentation detailing who I was, what I would do, and what I expected—as well as my non-negotiables. I included information

about what was important to me and my family. I found that sharing a little information about me and what I valued, including information about what was important to me and my family, not only gave the team a sense of who I was, it helped to begin building personal connections.

It is human nature when encountering something new or meeting a new boss to assume a "harm or value" mindset: Will this person or this new thing hurt me or help me? As a new leader, one of your first steps should be to address those fears. Let your team know why you are there, who you are, and what you expect while also fostering an atmosphere of opportunity. Part of this is helping the team understand how to get an A in your book by clearly communicating your expectations, how performance will be measured, and the active role you will play on the team. Start by giving your team clarity and candor, then follow up with ongoing and consistent communication.

In this context, promotions can be particularly challenging where team dynamics change and former coworkers become bosses. There is no simple answer for how to manage this apart from laying out your plan and sticking to your promises. Early in the process, however, team members will have to choose to come with you or leave. As Figure 15 illustrates, being half in (or half out) undermines the team through disengagement or outright sabotage, creating a passive-aggressive poison that, if not removed, will fester and impact everyone.

If you have received a promotion—even if you're the boss—respect and trust must still be earned. The simple act of giving these first will massively increase your odds of receiving them back in kind.

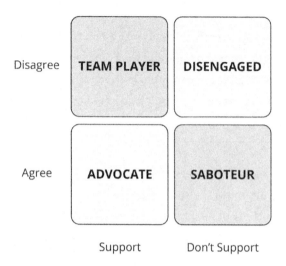

FIGURE 15 Individual's Engagement in a Decision Process

Listening

Listening may seem like such a simple concept, but true listening takes patience, effort, and a willingness to sometimes hold your tongue in service to the speaker. Everyone wants to be heard, and true listening—without appearing condescending, dismissive, or impatient—is a powerful way to create connection, build trust, and foster understanding and alignment through shared experience and dialogue, ultimately strengthening the fibers that hold a team together and improving outcomes. One of my favorite sayings regarding listening is, "feedback is a gift." In my experience, one of the best ways to offer feedback is to listen, openly and actively. Doing so can enable the speaker to "hear" themselves in new ways and often achieve new insights. Of course, feedback might be hard to receive, but thoughtful listening gives the speaker the best possible environment to reflect, process, and grow.

No doubt, you have witnessed conversations where an individual being criticized has then become defensive, offering excuses or rationales, or perhaps even going on the attack. A better approach in situations like this is almost always to ask and listen first. Put yourself in the shoes of the "accused" using empathy and genuine but candid questions. Even if the outcome for the individual is still net negative, you will learn more this way and are more likely to achieve a mutual understanding of the issues at hand without having to wade through the fog of defensiveness and hurt feelings that usually arise from the "interrogation" approach.

The Iceberg of Ignorance (Figure 16) is a term coined by Sidney Yoshida in 1989; it derives from a study he conducted on a cross-section of workers in a mid-size Japanese car manufacturing company to explore the disconnect between managers and front-line employees. Yoshida's study found that top-level management were aware of only 4 percent of the company's customer satisfaction problems, where 100 percent

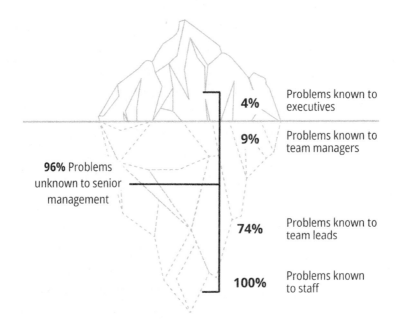

FIGURE 16 Based on 1989 study "The Iceberg of Ignorance"
by Sidney Yoshida

of front-line workers were aware of 100 percent of the problems. This was all due to poor communication in a strictly hierarchical leadership structure. In other words, while the front-line workers were getting an unfiltered earful from the customers every day, there was clearly a listening problem baked into the company hierarchy.

Most of the answers to the challenges a company faces can be found inside the teams if the leaders have the courage to listen, accept valid input, and use it to drive improvement or change.

There are many ways to "listen"; I have detailed a few below. Ultimately, you should find what works best for your situation, but until you feel you are doing too much listening, you are not doing enough.

Weekly 1:1 Calls with Your Direct Reports

While a clear cadence of calls with your direct reports may be logistically challenging or even seem unnecessary, I would argue that it is vital to make this cadence regular. Doing so can drive several important outcomes, particularly if you approach the sessions with a willingness to be vulnerable, give trust through what you share (without breaking the trust of others), establish a personal connection, understand what is happening in their universe, and show a willingness to share their burdens. Once you begin to know someone, their challenges will be easier to spot, from requests to cancel the meetings to the order of subjects to be discussed, or simply someone's mood.

I have found that the most productive meetings are based on a documented agenda, which should include items from the previous week, follow-ups on actions, key topics, decisions, what people are hearing within the company and in the market, and feedback. A best practice for organizing these meetings is to let the manager determine the cadence and time while the employee drives the agenda and topics.

Skip-Level Calls with Key People in Your Team

While it may be uncomfortable for your direct reports, a skip-level program with key staff members across your teams is a key tool for understanding what is happening across the organization. If you implement this as a recurring program and explain to your managers that it is out of your desire to promote a listening culture (vs. checking on them), your managers are likely to accept and even appreciate it as it will enable you to identify issues or opportunities they may have overlooked. Never use the information you glean to "ambush" your managers in any way as they could begin to block your access to your people. Feedback is a delicate resource that should be handled with openness, candor, and genuine care for the wellbeing of your teams.

I recommend a cadence of one per quarter for skip-level calls for key indirect employees, although your logistics may require this to be less frequent.

Brown Bag Lunches

For those unfamiliar, a brown bag lunch is a takeout or sandwich lunch informally shared around a table. Depending on the size of your team, if you have hundreds of employees within your purview, brown bag lunches can be a great tool for getting time with more people, normally individual contributors. The concept is simple and usually most effective in person, though I have successfully "brown-bagged it" virtually as well.

When traveling, I often took a light lunch in a meeting room with 10 to 15 individual contributors. These groups were usually a diverse cross-section of people, and I always began the meetings with the ground rules: (a) no managers, (b) no names recorded and feedback strictly confidential, (c) Chatham House rules (Vegas rules in the U.S.), (d) nothing's off the table, (e) I was there to listen and learn.

The amount of feedback I received in these informal sessions was incredible—truly a gift. Simple things like IT not getting a printer replaced or a broken coffee machine to larger issues like concerns about statutory requirements in certain countries. The power of this kind of session in giving everyone a voice manifested in exceptional employee NPS scores, improved engagement, a fantastic work ethic, and a higher sense of trust.

In the early days of taking on a North American team, I traveled across the country and held mini face-to-face townhall meetings over informal breakfasts with the different districts. Some of the assumptions made about decisions that were taken were surprisingly wrong and out of context. I was surprised at how misunderstood the company strategy and decisions were, and these meetings gave me an opportunity to correct these misunderstandings while building trust and learning from the teams so that my management team and I could improve.

Surveys

Most larger companies with established HR functions conduct some kind of annual survey. If this is the case in your company, make the most use of your survey. I've seen companies conduct surveys and then fail to communicate the results back to the team or make the information available in a constructive way for managers. While confidentiality must be ironclad, if the information a survey provides cannot be used, it is a waste of time and can be a real morale buster. If I am asked to complete a piece of work only to find it not used, I find it disrespectful of my time and effort, as if I'm being asked to talk and then not being listened to.

Beyond the annual company survey, I have used surveys extensively for all sorts of things, from competitions to naming new meeting rooms to feedback on a product or new sales process. I always began staff meetings with an open, around-the-table survey on a flip chart to find out what was important for the team to discuss, then closed the meetings reviewing whether we achieved their expectations and objectives. I often asked for feedback either in the moment or afterward on how to make things better. It is incredible how much you can learn when you ask; just be sure to provide feedback to the team to show them you value their input.

Construct your surveys thoughtfully. Asking the wrong questions or framing them poorly can be counterproductive. Also, consider how you will synthesize the data you receive. Sometimes a multiple-choice question is easier to parse and analyze than an open-ended one. I have also found that asking people to identify themselves can be very useful. I tend to offer a choice of anonymity, but the most actionable feedback comes from employees who identify themselves, even if they ask you to keep their feedback confidential. In a recent survey of about 200 people, I personally called about 45 respondents who had given me actionable feedback to thank them and promise my support. It was inspiring for them, and I felt a genuine groundswell of employee support as the word spread that I had done this.

Powerful Questions

Part of the journey of listening is learning to ask the right questions—or at least better ones. If you've ever heard a reporter receive yes and no answers from an interviewee, you will know how challenging this can be. Part of the challenge is learning to ask more open questions. For example, instead of, "Did you achieve your quota?" (and I bet you know the answer to this one), a more powerful question might be, "How does your quota attainment look?" You might then follow up with, "What could you do differently?" or, "What are your thoughts on how to change this?"

The idea here is to be aware of when a binary or yes/no question may feel confrontational or accusatory and may put someone in a defensive posture, which will always get in the way of getting good information. In the case above, the more open-ended question sets a tone of openness while allowing the person answering a little "wiggle room" to convey what is likely an uncomfortable truth. When you then follow up with a question about exploring options for improving, you are setting a tone of empathy and helping to create an environment of trust. Using this approach, you will get all the information you were after, and likely more, as the trust and empathy you can build with thoughtful questions both reinforces your leadership and sets the stage for candor in sharing sometimes uncomfortable information in a collaborative forum.

Communication and Direction Setting

A teacher of mine was fond of saying that we were given two ears and only one mouth, and we should use them in that ratio! Thus, listening in its various forms precedes communication in this discussion. What's more, listening should inform how you communicate and set direction.

Depending on your role within an organization, the content and style of your messages, and the direction you set with your team, will be instrumental in building your work "ecosystem." It is vital that your communication be sequenced appropriately and align with the overall message, culture, and tone your organization is working to deliver. In the following sections, I will lay out my communication cadence and what I try to achieve, which always aligns with the overall mission and cadence of my team and company.

Make no mistake, communication is one of the hardest parts of leadership. It is critical, strategic work, and we should always communicate in terms that make it possible for us to measure the outcomes of our messages. Promises made about meetings, trips, reviews, and teaming, for example, are promises that *must* be kept. Broken promises or a too-casual cadence will affect how you are seen, respected, and trusted. This does not mean that we must be inflexible and slaves to the plan, but when we do break cadence, we should clearly and logically communicate why. Changing the cadence every five minutes as a foil for poor organization (or some other leadership issue) will also never pass muster.

The Leadership Spine

In the human body, we know that damage to the spinal cord can compromise the signal from the brain to vital body functions, and vice versa, sometimes resulting in paralysis. In a similar way, in human organizations the connection between the most junior staff member and the CEO should be unobstructed and operate bidirectionally, with minimal interference. As you introduce functional layers into your organization, each new layer becomes a node along the organizational signal path, with the potential to change or stop those signals and paralyze all or part of the organization as a result.

In large organizations with thousands of employees and hundreds of managers, it is vitally important to control the strategic narrative with clear and structured communication plans. When you create a communication plan, every manager (and layer) in your organization should receive focused attention and explicit training on communication and leadership to ensure that messages from the top remain clear and actionable as they travel down—and back up—the organizational "spine." Put another way, the cadence from the top should be a clear drumbeat that even your customers and channel or business partners can march to.

When I was an employee, I generally wanted to *hear* from the CEO on key issues, but operationally, despite dozens of daily emails from other departments and informational white noise, I *listened* only for the voice, opinion, and mindset of my direct manager. The company's structured communication strategy gave me the confidence to tune out those other signals and still have the big picture.

If you are a leader in that management layer between CEO and first-line managers, consider carefully your role in communication and how you accentuate the CEO's message, and then deliver the pieces that your layer in the organization needs to focus on to ensure great outcomes. Redundant all-hands calls by every layer within the management chain can be extremely tedious for the team, so making the communication strategy a joined-up process can unlock real momentum. If you do not have a head of internal communication within your organization, someone who is in regular contact with every department driving alignment and building connective tissue on the communication strategy, please consider one as a strategic hire.

Change Management

The placement of this section is no accident. It is here because effective change management is predicated on good communication and listening. Whatever your plans for change may be, you will fail if you don't thoughtfully communicate that plan. Depending on which research you consult, somewhere between 50 and 70 percent of all organizational change initiatives fail. A number of critical steps are required in change management, and if you are about to manage a significant transformation in your business, I recommend that you seek out professional development such as subject matter experts and/or experienced mentors to reduce risk and improve your odds of success.

The following sections touch on a few key areas of change management that I have seen work and should prove useful for your journey.

Logic and Transparency Come First

When preparing a group for change, the first thing you need to do is explain why and develop a "case for change." In 1998, when I decided to move my family from Zimbabwe, I developed sound logic around the education prospects for our children, which included an assumption that they would eventually leave the country for global jobs. I established that the local currency was devaluing to a point where visiting our children, once they lived abroad, would become increasingly out of reach. My wife finally acceded to the change. Although it meant leaving her own extended family, she recognized that, for the future wellbeing of our family, moving was the best option.

Similarly, in your work environment, using logic and candor to build your case for change will more likely result in a reasonable plan that your people will be willing to follow. To be clear, this is not compulsory; in other words, you could just make the decision, deliver the plan, and move forward. But if you want a team to follow you, just like I wanted my wife to believe and follow me, you must give them clarity, logic, and the "why" so that they not only trust you but become powerful stakeholders in the journey.

Building the Plan

If you can build your case for change and it is powerful enough to establish support, the next step is to use this support to create your plan and workshop what the change will look like once completed. This is not something you need to—or should—do on your own. Frankly, even as a senior leader, you will not have considered all the pitfalls or every detail of your plan. That's where your team comes in. Working with a planning team will enable you to craft a vision and a clear set of measures that show what success looks like during the change process and after.

Throughout this process it is key to know your role. Start by leading your team through the problem statement and setting the direction for the work, then consider stepping back to allow your team to brainstorm and come back with solutions for your approval. This approach can be very powerful, both in terms of the more complete and actionable plan you end up with as well as the increased trust and productivity you will almost certainly receive from your team.

Executing on the Change Management Plan

The saboteur in Figure 15 was discussed as an individual who agreed with a plan but then disengaged or didn't support it through their actions. In change management, where belief and working to a common vision are so important, it is vital that you have complete buy-in from your entire team and that they support the process as true advocates. There is no room for "sabotage."

Change management can be extremely difficult, but it is made easier when you have the support of the whole team, from the board to the front office worker, and even your customers. At Symantec, we built the case for a major change to our go-to-market strategy so that we could share it with both customers and partners. In partner briefings, we asked for support, and over the next nine months, throughout our change process, the collaboration and support for the new vision was overwhelming. When you invite people with you on your journey, the results will often surprise you.

Annual Communication Plans

Effective communication—which should commence with the onset of the annual cycle—is more than just a process, it's a rhythmic cadence of ongoing information, giving teams clarity and avenues of engagement. While the spotlight often falls on Sales, this rhythm of communication is holistic, encompassing the entire company and providing a foundation that Sales can further refine and adapt for its stakeholders.

I've seen too many companies sporadically announce major events without context. They might unveil an annual strategy a couple of months into the fiscal year without tying all the ends together, leaving gaps in the narrative. This haphazard approach risks confusing the company's own workforce.

As senior leaders, we must internalize a crucial shift in perspective: We serve our teams. The vitality and dynamism of our organization are direct reflections of our leadership and communication approach. In the realm of Sales, it starts with transparently laying out the annual vision. It's not merely about presenting the plan but passionately advocating for its logic, ensuring that our team believes in its feasibility. Success lies in collective effort and unwavering dedication.

Every year in Sales, within the groups I was running and as close to day one as possible, we would begin the year with a clear and documented strategy for our team, including an annual plan that mapped out our overarching goals and how we planned to achieve them. I always tried to break these down into measurable chunks so that the teams could see a clear path to winning and believe that the goals we set were achievable. I am a big believer in the effectiveness of communicating with *why*, then *how*, and finally *what* we are going to do, and my communications would follow this simple formula.

In addition, with my management team I would build a document we called our "plan-on-a-page," detailing the vital few measures we had agreed would be our mantra and focus, along with the outcomes we were expecting. To do this we drew from our 6 Ps work to set the KPIs we'd focus on to deliver an outstanding result. The plan-on-a-page detailed role types and a clear set of priorities for each role as well as clear actions for each role to focus on, from Enterprise Sales to Mid-Market to Sales Engineering, etc.

On the back side of the plan, I added our company mission and values along with a clear sales process for deal reviews. I have always used the MEDDPICC[12] process, and I would include this along with what I would ask for in each step in the process so that every salesperson had a clear understanding of my expectations in deal reviews. This plan-on-a-page would be printed and laminated and provided to every person in Sales and adjacent teams (e.g., Marketing, Local Finance, Support, Consulting) so that it could serve as a constant reminder of how we would make our goal.

I started the year with a letter to the team explaining our current state and the challenges and opportunities before us. This went out to all team members, often with a small memento. Whenever possible, I would personalize these letters with a handwritten comment at the bottom asking for help or thanking the recipient for a memorable achievement. (Anecdotes and personalization count for a lot.) With the letter sent out to all staff members, we then conducted an all-hands kickoff call where I laid out the organizational structure, the teams, the roles, what I expected from each role, and a clear presentation of the plan-on-a-page along with the *how* in terms of execution.

---

12 Metrics, Economic Buyer, Decision Criteria, Decision Process, Paper Process, Implications of Pain, Champion, and Competition. Originally designed at Parametric Technology as MEDDIC and trademarked by Jack Napoli.

Naturally, every year we also had an annual kickoff meeting that encompassed training, enablement, and team building. I am a huge proponent of doing this in person as it is the one time in the fiscal year when teams can really come together for quality enablement, energizing, and "winding up" to go out and deliver a great year. The challenge with kickoffs, however, is that logistics affect timing, and usually these large events would happen in the second month of the fiscal year. As such, I would always decouple my annual communication plan so that I could release it as close as possible to day one of the year. That way our communications in the kickoff could build on and dovetail with the already "launched" year and plan that the team would hopefully have bought into by that time. This also got around the perennial problem of teams waiting for kickoff to share vital information, losing time, and wasting an opportunity to move faster.

Half-Year Communication

Fear of change and choppy decision-making on strategy and direction can make for a very unsettled environment and poor execution. Fortunately, the year's halfway point provides an opportunity to tweak the execution plans for the year. In my career, I achieved my most successful multiyear strategies by "pausing for thought" in months six and seven of each fiscal year and then informally communicating with key leaders where I thought the following year was going to go. In addition, in months five and six, I would share ideas around structure, promotions, capability, and planning. I did this both to read the teams' reactions to my ideas as well as to stimulate and solicit feedback (confidentially, where appropriate). As a result, the teams were seldom surprised by announcements, and they felt like stakeholders in the process.

Structured listening techniques and informal feedback made developing the strategy for the next fiscal year highly productive and extremely positive for the team, as involving them from the half-year mark fostered a sense of agency and buy-in that ultimately drove us all to better outcomes.

Quarterly Communication

The most successful leaders I have worked with employed a system of quarterly communications and all-hands calls. Below is an outline of quarterly tools I have used.

1. A Post-Quarter Note

Normally, within an hour past midnight of the quarter close I drafted a one- or two-page account of the latest quarter end and the journey that brought us there. This often included stories of great deals won, anecdotes of great accomplishments, and honest accounts of where we may have failed or needed to improve. I called out and thanked people, acknowledged the contributions of other departments, and encouraged everyone to begin the cycle again. The note would go out to my team as well as to all the leaders of supporting functions and other management team members directly involved in the business. Everyone wants to participate in the success or the learning at the end of the quarter, and whether directly in Sales or not, involving as many people as possible, as recipients or even part of the narrative, builds amazing spirit and shared commitment.

This note was particularly useful in driving the team to greater levels of execution. And because it explained to the entire company how we were doing, it gave other leaders from different departments an opportunity to send personal notes to high achievers or those who had shown valiant effort. One particularly good quarter, I delivered a personal "note" to the finance department when I snuck out of my global senior leadership meeting to share a glass of champagne with them for the part they had played. They rarely received kudos and were incredibly grateful for the recognition of their effort.

2. A Quarterly All-Hands Call

In every company I've worked for, the CEO would deliver an all-hands call around the third week of the quarter. On these calls, the CEO would typically reinforce the strategy, drive a call to action in a specific area, ensure alignment on key goals, and bring in executives to reinforce key messages. A portion of the call was also reserved for celebrating performances, sharing information, and giving awards.

As a sales leader, paying close attention to key messages and direction from the CEO is vital. Taking your cues from the CEO and conducting your own all-hands calls is very important, and finding a good (and humane) cadence of all-hands communications is key to acceleration and success. By contrast, I've seen a company hold major meetings every day for a solid week—the CEO Wednesday, the CRO Thursday, the geo VP Friday, the regional leader the following Monday, and the country or district manager Tuesday. Imagine how that team felt!

Balancing the right amount of communication to motivate, inspire, and align execution is key. The first thing I would ask you as a leader is, "Why do you need a call in the first place?" Is it just because you are a senior person with an itch to do an all-hands, or does it add value? And how will it be different from the other calls you just heard? Could you perhaps swap it with a "fireside chat" or a Q&A session for your team rather than a full-blown call? What will make the biggest impact? It is not a checklist or a cascading requirement for all teams to do a call if it is not necessary. Planning and collaboration between leadership teams, picking up on different messages, or adapting the call to action locally may differentiate your messages. And when calls are synchronized, they can be exceptionally powerful, showing the unity of the management team in driving cadence, alignment, and a "one team" approach, whatever the individual contributor's role may be in the company.

I learned a long time ago that most people listen to two leaders first: their manager and their CEO. If you fall between these two roles, your main jobs in quarterly communication are to influence the CEO's communication to ensure that your teams' priorities and results are seen and acknowledged, and to direct your first-line managers to ensure that the teams are coming with you on the journey. Of course, your communications are important too, just know that you don't need to communicate everything. Lean into influencing, coaching, and directing, and communicate to set direction and reinforce a common strategy.

3. A Quarterly Managers' Call

A key part of the journey with my managers was a quarterly all-hands call with me. As a CRO (chief revenue officer) and as an SVP overseeing many hundreds of employees, I also set the foundation for good communication by insisting that I personally interview every manager we hired. This gave me the opportunity to talk about culture and values and make sure that the candidate would be able to align and communicate in a way that was a good fit for our organization. I then ensured, through my quarterly managers' call, that there was dialogue and continued building of the culture. In the context of communication, having the right ratio of managers and communicating with them is crucial.

Having quarterly all-hands calls with only managers created a forum where messages were sharper and more mature, and a clear set of management topics could be offered for discussion, feedback, and planning for further communication to the wider team. It is worth repeating that

> Every manager and every layer within an organization can be an enabler or a blocker. In the children's game "telephone," a message is whispered from one kid to another in a line, and by the time the message travels from one end of the line to the other, it has invariably completely changed. In the same way, messages can become distorted as they pass from various managers through layers in the organization, colored by culture and communication style and skill. As a leader, it is vital that you work hard to align and clarify messages at every layer.

people listen to two leaders first, their manager and the CEO, so as the CRO, I made sure that I was aligned with the CEO and that our managers were coached and equipped to speak with one voice and equipped with the tools to sharpen and harmonize their messages.

I generally conducted my quarterly managers' calls a week or so after the CEO's all-hands calls. This gave the managers time to get feedback from their teams and form questions around the previous quarter's performance and the next quarter's action plan.

Finally, I've learned that assumption is a powerful enemy of speed, teaming, and execution, so I never assumed our teams understood the decisions we made or the reasons for any of our actions. I always double checked, listened for questions, and repeated myself, making sure that my messages were not only clear but foundationally understood in terms of not only the *what*, but also the *why* and the *how*.

4. Monthly

Due to the nature of high-tech businesses and the cadence of teams at various levels, my monthly meetings were normally departmental or administrative. We conducted strategy and direction setting quarterly, and the operation of the business was weekly. Our monthly meetings were therefore usually interdepartmental and executive management.

As such, communications were not necessarily organized monthly. I make this point to give you pause to think about your business and what you need to be successful within your own environment. Your cadence will change based on your role and level within the organization.

5. Weekly

As a leader, my weekly communication has evolved greatly over time, and my communication style has changed dramatically based on region, role, and constituency.

When I was director of a region with numerous district managers reporting to me over a widely distributed geography, I held a 90-minute weekly all-hands call to celebrate wins, share ideas, invite guest speakers, and generally keep connected. Some critics suggested this was a little too much, but I kept it light and informative, giving over about a third of the time to constituents to share wins and best practices—and it worked! The community grew close and collaborative even though many of them met face-to-face just once a year.

As a VP with around 300 people working for me, I had to change my style. I needed to step back to allow the local directors to run their businesses, but at the same time I needed to find a way to remain connected without interfering in daily management. A video blog became my go-to tool, and I would record quick 30-second clips when I was in a different country or at a customer event or with partners. I talked about what was important, about wins, and about culture, and I made sure that the cultural thread was always there to bring the team together. Cell phones make this approach drop-dead easy, both on the recording and viewing ends, but if this is not your style, even an end-of-week email will mean a lot to your team.

As an SVP and again as a CRO, with over 1,000 in my team, my style needed to change again, and I reduced the number of video blogs to more strategic communications about once a month. Still, I always tried to send a short email to the team on Fridays reviewing the week. Though I'm sure many skipped it, many others appreciated it and found it useful, and for those who needed to feel connected, it was always there.

Global and Regional Differentiation

While living in Dubai, I was fortunate to experience a mix of cultures. Most working there were expatriates, and it was a real melting pot for motivated people willing to leave home and strike out for their future. Working for a multinational showed me the massive diversity in regional teams, politics, bureaucracy, and in how things got done.

There are important differences between the two largest global economic zones, North America and Europe, in terms of culture, decision-making, and leadership style, and new CROs or global leaders who either misunderstand or discount these differences can set teams back and unnecessarily create trust issues or slow momentum. For example, I've known European leaders who saw the U.S. as one country to sell into. But the northeast U.S. sales environment is not like the Midwest, which is even more unlike the southeast, and while Americans share many unifying cultural qualities, from a sales perspective these different regions may as well be different countries. Similarly, I've seen executives in the U.S. who lack global experience fail to comprehend the challenges in Europe, whose varied politics, currencies, culture, and languages pose their own challenges.

"The Middle East is not a country," one of my team members said while briefing a European leadership team meeting. It was funny at the time, but it conveys a key message about the importance of assumptions and understanding local issues. As a sales leader of a regional market, part of my job was to educate my global leadership about local challenges. When I lived in the Middle East, I would buy books as gifts for my global leaders to give them insight into the regional differences. Fridays were a day of rest, for example, so organizing all-hands calls on Friday was hardly sympathetic to the culture.

I have also observed sales teams trying to take advantage of naive management teams who are *too* accommodating. They may tell their HQ that their region is different and then try to shortcut the sales process, find ways to avoid accountability, or ask for different funding models. Conversely, I have seen a complete lack of empathy in global teams that fail to understand local sensitivities or issues. Knowing "how things work" in local cultures is vital in setting global strategy and executing effectively. It takes time, trust, and collaboration between leaders and teams across time zones and continents to succeed.

Important cultural and regional differences abound around the world. Some European countries place a high importance on detailed and specific roadmaps for products and sticking to three-year plans (something many technology companies forget when chopping and changing features or sunsetting products). In the Far East, entering markets can be particularly challenging—or nearly impossible—without the sponsorship and support of a local partner. In some countries, early adoption is higher. In others, inside sales is more effective. In some major markets, it may be acceptable to simply sell a product over the phone where in others a proof of concept or a local face-to-face meeting is expected.

Cloud and SaaS products present both opportunities and challenges with regional differentiation. Data rights and data location are becoming more of an issue, and while technologists and engineering teams are pushing companies to single data centers in key locations, many companies now require that data be stored in-country. Moving to a Pareto model—focusing on the "easiest" eight out of ten countries—can address much of this, but those final two countries will demand more careful planning. Data privacy requirements in countries like Japan will be challenging, as will FedRAMP in the U.S., as you build your go-to-market strategy.

Local customs and culture also play a major role in meeting customer needs. In the early 2000s, in a negotiation with a high-level government leader in a Middle Eastern country, I suggested that we build a security operations center in one location to support multiple countries in the Middle East. I naively thought that this would create critical mass and improve the client's security posture. Objectively, it would have, but culturally each country would have wanted the operations center on their soil and would not have been keen to collaborate due to local cultural and political issues.

In another strategic planning process, we analyzed major global software companies and determined that 80 percent of their bookings were from about a dozen countries. As the percentage moved up, fewer than 50 countries contributed more than 95 percent of bookings. With roughly 225 countries in the world and most bookings coming from a fraction of that number, our analysis clearly pointed to the need for more strategic planning and resource allocation. There is also an incredible opportunity to drive more channel-centric go-to-market strategies in foreign countries where reinvesting in local economies could be a "good look" while moving operating expenses to a variable cost model and avoiding local challenges and the legal burden of owning entities.

Global companies are increasingly shifting to more semi-franchised models outside their core markets.

Awareness, good counsel, and sensitivity to local issues can help you avoid mistakes and create a much better experience and value as you build your sales team. Most people I've met in business, regardless of where they came from, fundamentally understand that an authentic, low-ego, respectful approach works everywhere. Get a good coach or mentor with local knowledge and you will be positioned well to succeed.

Embrace Diversity

When I lived in Dubai and ran an office there, I had the privilege of building a team from just 3 people to well over 150 in the space of just a few years. In Dubai, expert staff were mainly brought in on expatriate contracts, so I was careful to ensure that we didn't over-index on any one group, nationality, gender, or demographic. By the time we'd grown to about 50 people, our team reflected over 24 nationalities and an extraordinary level of diversity. The results were evident in an abundance of new ideas, different points of view, and genuine *esprit de corps* as everyone felt valued and a part of something bigger. We would never have achieved this if, when building the team, we had favored one group over another. There is power in diversity, which elevates everyone's game and breaks down barriers.

In many countries this may be more complicated, but stating your goals clearly at the outset about diversity and inclusion will create a platform for others to follow. Consider the following:

1. **Diversity in Hiring**: Insist on a diverse mix of resumes from your talent team. If, for example, you want to improve gender diversity,

you will have to ensure that the way you proceed both attracts the people you are looking for and includes the diversity you are planning for. In a simple first step, I created a rule that when looking at candidates for positions, I refused to review a set of resumes without a minimum mix of diverse candidates. This forced a change in behavior throughout the hiring process.

2. **Avoiding Gender Bias**: Tools to avoid gender bias in hiring and advertising were the next important steps. One of the CISOs I worked with coached me and helped me understand how gender bias in job advertisements, down to the words used to describe roles, could put people off applying. I was horrified but relieved to learn that software and tools are available to help overcome this and make the company and the role you are hiring for more appealing to a wider, more diverse group.

3. **Promoting Strategically**: Promote using equal opportunity frameworks. A balanced leadership team will attract talent. It may seem obvious, but it is surprising how many middle-aged, white, male leadership teams expect other genders or groups to want to work with them. When setting up a call center some time ago, we took the opportunity to invest in top female leaders, and this resulted in a rush of CVs from female applicants.

4. **Grassroots Investing**: Invest in programs with schools and universities to bring in early-stage talent. I was lucky enough to work in a large team at one of my employers who had invested in corporate social responsibility initiatives supporting local girls' schools with career days. This included field trips to our offices, where the students could see what it was like to work in a software company, helping to break down perceived barriers and kindling interest. I'm also a strong supporter of graduate programs as a way to encourage

diversity. Real progress can be made with a grassroots approach, even if it brings just a few people on board. Every small step makes a difference.

Collaboration

Working in the Middle East really drove home to me the need for collaboration. Video conferencing became a key tool for us (a good decade before Covid), and with Dubai literally half a world away from California, it was hugely important to interlock and drive collaboration not only within our team but between all our departments.

As a result, my interactions and personal relationships with many of the executives in HQ grew tighter and more proactive than what they experienced with many of their colleagues within their own state. In some ways our very isolation from other global teams made us more proactive and understanding of the value of communication, trust, collaboration, and relationships (a great many of which are going strong after more than 20 years).

A great example of this collaboration was exhibited by one of our key sales reps in Saudi Arabia. The market had gone through considerable change by the mid-2000s, and large, lucrative software deals in cybersecurity were available to companies who could deliver outcomes that our customers needed. The rep built a basic template, which was similar to a pitch deck you might see a startup using today. The template included the opportunity, a problem statement, key stakeholders, revenue potential, headwinds, tailwinds, risks, and rewards as well as an action plan with stakeholders around the world. The rep's secret sauce were his updates and weekly sync-ups, where staff from varying departments could hear how he was progressing and enjoy a moment of thanks and praise for progress made. When deals were won, the celebration was truly a team event, and his ability to inspire teamwork and communicate globally made him incredibly successful.

The key here is that everyone wants to be part of something, and sharing a little of your success with the people who help make it possible not only brings joy and a feeling of participation, it also cements relationships and builds strong foundations that can withstand difficulties and hard times when outcomes are less positive. Relationships, trust, and bringing people with you on your journey are all fundamental to success. True leadership is not built on the backs of others, it is celebrated as those you collaborate with raise you up.

Inspirational Leadership

During my time at Symantec, I had the privilege of working with some amazing leaders. My first CEO, John W. Thompson, joined the company a few months before me, and during my induction training he came and addressed the new hires. His words back in 1999 resonate today as they did then: "We are building the world's most important cybersecurity company, polishing it from a diamond in the rough and helping it emerge in all its brilliance." This was the mission I vigorously joined him on, and his words energize me still today!

Inspirational leadership can take many forms, but to truly inspire a team, authenticity and consistency must be at the core. At Symantec, I was inspired by the mission and the shared opportunity to create something very special. These were the sparks that lit the flame, but the inspiration that kept it burning came from the passion, loyalty, and authentic leadership that I received from my manager and the leaders around me.

When leading a team in London, one of my sales team called me on a Friday at 1:00 p.m. At the time I was a good 90 minutes outside the city running planning sessions on my computer, casually dressed in jeans and a golf shirt. He said, "Kevin, we have the opportunity to meet one of the key strategy team members for a large global bank, face-to-face. He is here from New York for the day. I know it's a long shot but is there any chance you are around?" Without hesitation, I replied, "Give me two hours and I'll be there." I quickly cleaned up, put on my best suit and tie, jumped on a train, and (with a little running) was there by 3:00. It was a great meeting, but the most amazing thing was that by ditching my schedule with no notice to show up on a Friday afternoon, I said more to my teams about commitment than I could have any other way. Inspirational leadership is all about walking the talk and leading from the front.

Mission

My journey over the past 35 years really became turbo charged when I was able to attach myself to the mission of the company I was working for and identify with its core values and goals. We all strive for a sense of purpose, a sense that we are building a legacy and that our combined efforts are more than the individual parts. The harsh realities of corporate life and of PE and VC firms with their playbooks and valuation-based outcomes can be challenging at times, but they are not necessarily in conflict with this altruistic perspective.

There are three key groups within any company environment, and the mission, the vision, and the team must equally embrace all three if they are to succeed. They are:

- **Shareholders and owners**, whose investments must be protected
- **Employees**, whose wellbeing must be paramount
- **Customers**, whose outcomes must be guaranteed as best as possible

The list is not numbered as order is not important. This is a "virtuous circle," where each group must be equally respected.

Shareholders and owners will naturally be looking for maximum return on their investment. They may or may not be investing money and/or time in the company for altruistic reasons, but their investment is as critical to the success of the company as any other group, and our job as leaders is to help them achieve a good (or better) return.

The life blood of any company is its employees, and the extent to which this group is able to work in a dynamic, equitable, and well-rewarded culture is the extent to which your company will thrive. All too often I have seen shareholder decisions or senior management decisions that favor short-term profit or selfish objectives at the expense of the employee. This not only negatively impacts medium-term results, it can breed damaging trust issues that are felt for many years. In turn, employees should consider shareholders and customers in their assessments of what is fair and reasonable, a mindset that generally results when leadership builds effective communication strategies, collaborates, and establishes transparency and trust.

Of course, without customers, your company would not exist, and challenging yourself every day to do your very best for your customers is what separates average outcomes from the extraordinary. It is important to remember that customers have choices, and creating an environment where they choose you takes hard work and commitment. Consistently delivering great outcomes that exceed their expectations will create the loyalty you need to be successful.

This does *not* mean "the customer is always right." There is a balance among the three stakeholder groups that is absolutely vital in creating symbiotic relationships where every party can win. In many situations I have had to challenge customers on their approach to my employees or in their unreasonable expectations around costs. Normally, when working with customers, honest and transparent communication, empathy, and sensible perspectives create a foundation for great outcomes. When facing a customer who is negotiating hard, it may seem easier to capitulate on a negotiation point for short-term cash flow or a commission check, but the downstream ramifications of bad faith negotiations and short-sighted capitulations can be long lasting and harmful.

> While working with a startup supplying a large global bank with strategic technology, requests for customizations and extras got so great that we eventually recorded a loss on the project. The pressure to get the deal and the desperation for cash flow led us deeper and deeper into a dysfunctional relationship as the customer realized how much we needed them. Great account management is vital in managing critical relationships to ensure that the deals done are good for everyone.

Mission is a complex topic. While the words in the mission around key stakeholders may seem straightforward—and arguably should be—the actions we take to achieve alignment can involve a lot of detail and dedication. When we talk about mission in this context, we are not just talking about the company's mission statement or fiscal imperative. It is also the more personal mission we are on every day. A government may have a mission to defend sovereign territory, but when a soldier is tasked with taking a hill or defending a bridge, that mission also becomes very much about *them and their team*. In my leadership journey, I have found those "bridges" to take the form of short-term, achievable goals and sometimes even more altruistic objectives like supporting worthy causes in a local community. Fostering a sense of accomplishment and contribution can be massively inspiring and can unlock deeper levels of commitment within a team.

I strongly recommend *Start with Why: How Great Leaders Inspire Everyone to Take Action*, by Simon Sinek.[13] This book can help you tap into both your *why* and your customers' *why* as a way to make your teams' inspirational journeys more relevant and your customer interactions more meaningful.

Creativity

In a high-performing sales organization, creativity and freedom of thought and expression are not just visible, they are actively encouraged. If you've ever walked into an office and seen smiling faces and curious teams with lots of ideas, you probably immediately sensed the energy and latent potential. Or maybe you've seen the opposite: workplaces where no one looks up from their desk and there is a feeling of isolation and morbid bureaucracy. Even in environments that require silence and focus, you can feel this difference. At the beginning of this chapter, I discussed Maslow's hierarchy of needs, where self-actualization sits at the top of the triangle. In this context, when you give your teams creative freedom, they can begin to realize their full potential.

To be clear, creativity is not limited to the arts. In business, it may be a talent for innovatively crafting mega deals, solving tough customer problems, or finding novel ways to grow the business to new heights or in new areas. The challenge is that, as with any environment where people work in teams, relationships matter, and the concepts of safety and belonging that Maslow championed are vital to unlocking the creativity we all need to be extraordinary. It only takes a moment or a single event to damage a relationship, destroy that safety, and snuff out the atmosphere of freedom you have cultivated for creativity, but if

13 Portfolio/Penguin, 2009, New York.

those relationships are grounded in authenticity and a genuine desire to see your entire team succeed, odds are the creative spark will survive the inevitable challenges and occasional high emotion of any dynamic workplace.

During my career, I have always tried to create a balanced office environment, one where process, rules, business culture, and a competitive spirit are all cultivated and respected—while creativity is also encouraged. Some of the most creative sessions I've participated in have been in moments where emotions are heightened, or where need has forced an issue. I remember a quarterly review in Hungary with my extended team after a particularly brutal quarter. Without pointing to any specific individual, we took a hard look at ourselves and asked, "Is this what good looks like?" We were not happy with what we saw in the mirror, but our collective disappointment stirred a new creative energy, and we were able to come up with new ways to drive change and improve execution. Without a business culture that supported this kind of creative problem solving, we'd never have had the latitude to improve our performance.

Of course, success can also be an opportunity for creativity. Sometimes that can come in the form of simply documenting how you achieved a particularly notable win (or wins) by creating a repeatable process. Seen another way, this is a way of tapping the energy that is often a byproduct of great success. In successful months or quarters where momentum and energy are high, use that energy to build those repeatable processes and document how you are winning. This is how we built the 6 Ps (see section *Aligning to the 6 Ps)*. It was a winning season and we were laser focused. We used the tangible energy and clarity this brought to document our processes, which we then repeated time and again, sustaining our momentum even in the hard times.

Creativity can be borne out of unexpected situations as well. In Oman, at a senior staff retreat, I went for an early bite with my team soon after we arrived. This was hard on the heels of a particularly brutal business review with my manager, and I was really struggling to find a way forward. Still, I worked hard to keep my emotions away from the team, hoping that our meeting would yield some ideas. Bounding into the room with an infectious smile and unbridled optimism, one of the leaders exclaimed how excited he was about our opportunity to change the world as a team and how inspired he was to be working with me. His words, enthusiasm, and perspective were like warm sunshine on a cold day, and for a moment I chose to believe him. By the end of our third day, we had created a plan that gave us one of our most successful years ever. This experience taught me that even when I'm down I should always be open to others who *are* energized and are operating high up the triangle of the Maslow hierarchy. Let their infectious energy help you unlock your own.

Difficult Conversations

Early in my leadership career I was instructed by my manager to fire a manager who worked for me. We were restructuring our business and planning for the next phase of our growth, and this individual had not jelled with the team, and his results, while reasonable, were inconsistent and mediocre. Change was needed, and deep down I knew this, but I lacked the courage and depth of experience to follow through. Luckily, I had a manager who knew what to do, and he advised me to restructure and remove the individual in question.

I agonized over this, picturing the manager's family and his situation, and I was desperate not to hurt him. But it had to be done, so the issue moved quickly from *what* to do to *how*. These are two distinct phases—making the decision and then executing on it—and both have their challenges. In this situation my manager helped with the initial decision, but I still agonized over the consequences for the individual. So, I planned the meeting meticulously, documenting my words, involving HR, and even making a schedule around how I would advise my team and communicate to the larger organization. I lost sleep playing out the different outcomes. Finally, the day came when I delivered the news, and while it was tough, the manager was clearly relieved; he knew as well as I that it was not working. When I spoke to my team, their only question was, "What took you so long?"

In another situation, a trusted team member began to make some negative comments in meetings and refused to execute on some key projects. As a leader, I had the option to either react to this individual's insubordination and potentially cause stress and unnecessary damage within the team or try to understand what had precipitated his unusual behavior. I called him and asked first if he was facing any specific challenges or if anything was wrong. I wanted to lead with empathy but also let him know that his attitude needed adjustment. Talking to him I learned that he was just doing too much—he was exhausted. After a couple of days, he told me that he was grateful that I had challenged him and taken the time to have a direct conversation to clear the air. Ultimately, he came around and was more energized than ever.

Difficult conversations are an interesting part of leadership. As a rule, I am unaccommodating of poor excuses and mediocrity, but caring deeply about my people has enabled me to have the toughest of conversations, drive extremely high levels of discipline, and set incredibly high standards. If you can do this, your team will follow you to the ends of the earth. As a leader, it is better to resist the opportunity to react, no matter how enticing it may be. Consider your responses before you make them and consider the knock-on effects of your actions. The unintended consequences of a rash outburst or decision can be far reaching.

Gut Feel

Gut feel is where intuition *plus* experience combine to provide guidance. It is probably one of the most important tools you have as you grow in experience as a leader. In the *Science* chapter, we learned about the ladder of inference, where a lack of good data creates the potential for poor decisions based on incorrect assumptions. While an objective, data-based approach to decision-making is foundational, strictly information-driven decisions risk ignoring the valuable intuition, heart, and *gut* that can only come from experience. Finding a good balance can be challenging.

Self-awareness is a key component of my gut feel. I am an optimist and I lean toward trust first, so I seek contrarian views from others who are able to assess and see things that I have not yet seen. When my gut is the only "information" I have, these people are invaluable at helping me form an opinion. The first among my many advisors is my wife of more than 30 years. When discussing someone she knows, her point of view is unfailingly concise and crystal clear. She has a gift for seeing to the heart of things, and while she always sees the good in others, she is equally shrewd at seeing what is really happening.

> "In the multitude of counselors there is safety." These words from Proverbs are as true now as ever. I am lucky to have a great group of people around me whom I often ask for advice and opinions. I don't always like what they have to say, but over the years I've learned to trust the wisdom of the group.

Never act on gut feel alone or with impunity. Where data fails to point the way (or does so unconvincingly), take guidance, lean on your experience, listen to as many voices as you can, and then make a decision you can stand behind. Just remember, the responsibility for your decision is all yours, regardless of the outcome or who told you to do it!

What then *How* then *Who*

Some of my friends will smile at the title of this section as these three words—in this order—have been at the heart of many decisions, reorganizations, and discussions in my career. The sequence has proven invaluable in driving great outcomes. When planning change or creating a strategy, understanding *what* you are trying to achieve before deciding *how* seems logical, but too often I've seen blind execution (how) happen before a plan (what), and people be chosen for roles (who) before an org chart (what) is decided, each with predicably bad results. Breaking the sequence can be dangerous.

The challenge with getting this sequence right often arises from personal feelings for individuals or an attempt to build a plan around people you care for. While outwardly noble, this approach can put the entire organization at risk. I found this particularly true when I was building teams in small, emerging markets. While we were part of a larger company, there were always small teams on the ground with good people desperate for more responsibility and bigger job titles. I see the same thing in some startups today, where a company of 100 people has more vice presidents than salespeople, resulting in competing management priorities, too much supervision, not enough execution, and ultimately poor execution, dysfunction, frustration, and the loss of top performers.

The best way to conduct a logical decision-making process is to start with a clear and concise description of *what* you are trying to achieve.

Presenting the *what* to a team and brainstorming the *how* together can then be a fun, productive, and motivating exercise, one that results in buy-in and even some of the *who* getting decided.

Insight: Tell Me What I Don't Know!

Insight is the understanding of a specific cause and effect within a particular context. The term insight can have several related meanings:

- *A piece of information*
- *The act or result of understanding the inner nature of things or of seeing intuitively*
- *An introspection*
- *The power of acute observation and deduction, discernment, and perception*
- *An understanding of cause and effect based on the identification of relationships and behaviors within a model, context, or scenario*[14]

In a senior management meeting I attended some years ago, I was reviewing product and pricing information with my product management colleagues. We had been struggling with the sales in some of the product lines and were having a hard time getting at the cause. In frustration, one of my colleagues asked me, "What is it that you want?" I replied, "Tell me something I don't know!" We invest an incredible amount of time in creating data, and most companies have more reports than they could ever consume—but very few have true insight.

Over more than 30 years in commercial roles, I can probably count on two hands the number of operational professionals I've known who

14 Source – Wikipedia

could parse and correlate data in a way that yielded useful insight into what was happening in a process or product line. The absence of insight makes taking action or making decisions extremely challenging as the outcomes become more hopeful than predictable.

Remember the phrase, "Are you good or are you lucky?" Of course, "good" breaks down into attitude, ability to execute, and a number of other factors, but I can tell you that a lack of clear, actionable insight is a sure-fire way to miss—even if you are good.

In my personal journey, I have always tried to find positive and curious people who have a deep knowledge of the business and the segment we are pursuing, along with great business intelligence skills and an ability to visualize. People with these specific insight skills are hard to find, but they are critical in accelerating success as it is often not the skill or the will of your people that is challenged, but the lack of a clear path to success. In our small business segment in the mid-2000s, a colleague of mine was responsible for the segment. Using Excel, he managed to break down sales by end user company, product, reseller, license type— basically in every way possible—and after studying this data for a few days, he was able to pick up on a trend pointing to more than half of our challenges being in a specific product line where customers had bought between 50 and 75 licenses. We then called down to customers and partners to better understand their buying decisions. Based on what we learned, we then changed our pricing bands, our support, and most importantly the margins for our small business resellers, which had tapered off above 50 user licenses. Without my colleague's insight from the data, we might have restructured, changed out the manager, or rolled the dice on some other decision; instead, we managed to grow that segment three times faster than we had thought possible.

If you find you lack the sufficient raw data to develop actionable insights, go to the source! Reach out to your customers and partners directly and talk to them. Insight ultimately comes from asking powerful questions and going to where the data resides.

Balance

One of the most fundamental requirements in the art of leadership is balance. Finding balance in your priorities, in your management style, in your work/life balance, and in the things you control can be extremely challenging. Like a bicycle wheel where each spoke is a priority in your life, if any one spoke loosens or breaks, the wheel risks becoming out of balance. One or two spokes out of whack may be manageable, but one too many can send you over the handlebars.

We are all different in how we prioritize and structure our days. Some of us are morning people, others may do their best work at midnight. Whatever your stye, it is important to prioritize your time in sync with your daily rhythms. For example, if I don't exercise first thing in the morning, it doesn't happen. To balance my days I built a small checklist I call the 6 Fs. I strive for a good balance between fitness, family, friends, finance, faith, and fun. I believe that to have professional balance you must have balance in your personal life.

To be sure, the path to balancing your professional life can be laid with traps. You may find yourself in a new role where you feel you need to work harder to show you are worthy of the promotion. Maybe the person you backfilled in your old position isn't cutting it, and you feel responsible for helping out. Even seasoned leaders can be tripped up by common events like surprise requests for board meeting presentations, unscheduled business reports, or sudden travel demands. To push back on unreasonable asks you must come from a place of balance. This starts with understanding what is important and planning time for every detail of your day, week, month, and quarter.

Planning your 30-day and 90-day cadence will help you immensely with achieving balance. Be sure to program in time to step back and think; all action with no reflection counts for at least two "broken spokes!" In times of crisis these planned sessions will help separate you from the "fog of war" and give you some breathing space above the battlefield to consider your priorities.

Finally, surround yourself with people who give you energy and "oxygen." I am a serial optimist and I tend to exude energy with my teams and with the people I lead, but this requires energy, and I factor recharge time into my cadence. When you face difficulties and barriers, you need people around you who can support you and give you hope and encouragement. I can't count the times an encouraging word or positive remark from my team has made all the difference—a much needed spark that kept my fires burning in overwhelming times.

Offsite Meetings, Events, and Reward Trips

Over the years I have attended hundreds—maybe thousands—of offsite meetings in some form or another. Organizing, planning, and executing them is easy (less "art" and more process). But the reason this section is in the *Art* chapter of the book is that I want you to think about meetings and other events less as tactical gatherings to exchange information and attend seminars and workshops (again, process), and more as memorable experiences where teams can find energy, inclusion, and a sense of real connection.

Offsite Meetings

I have been extremely fortunate to be a part of or to lead many teams throughout my career. During that time I've learned that the real magic in a team—the trust, momentum, and energy—happens when everyone on the team is in one place, together, off site. Some of my oldest professional relationships formed during offsite meetings or training courses, and some of my greatest team challenges were overcome around a campfire. It's during those side meetings and after dinner informal gatherings when people really communicate and build lasting relationships.

Ethics in Offsite Meetings

Throughout my career in international sales, I have witnessed many bad decisions and embarrassing moments at staff events. I could fill another book with the stories (you won't read any here). When high-performance teams congregate, it's like an open flame at a gas station. Take care not to let it get away from you.

One of the quickest ways to destroy a team or a great culture is to ignore or overlook ethical standards or fail to set a good example. Get ahead of any potential challenges, make sure you are clear in your expectations, and review them with your teams, both in person and in writing. My approach was to speak to my management team about everything— from showing up on time to interpersonal respect to personal brand and reputation. I even coached my team about sitting up front in worldwide conferences, dress code, and reaching out to other senior leaders. Offsite meetings are not an opportunity to party, although after-hours get-togethers can help with team building when done right. Offsites are career-building and networking opportunities and a chance to shine. Make sure your teams are crystal clear on their ethical guidelines, down to the minutest detail.

Team Building at Offsites

When preparing an offsite, it is advisable to program time into the schedule for team-building activities designed to enhance trust, remove barriers, and create a sense of teamwork that can then be carried through to the work the team does going forward.

Team building can take many forms, from simple games to activities like hiking in the mountains to programs or events that deliver value within communities. I favor activities or events that benefit communities because they almost always deliver value both to the company and to the groups in need. The optics for these events are important. For your teams and business culture, they help build a sense of duty and care for the wider community. And when done thoughtfully and sincerely—not just "window dressing"—they can raise your business profile in the local community.

Many local charities will have platforms or programs for companies to participate, normally involving a monetary donation along with a commitment of volunteer hours to contribute in a way that makes volunteers feel personally invested. I have always been careful to find causes with proper registration and bona fide credentials, ensuring that our relationship is transparent and ethically above board. The most successful events I have seen were those where teams could collaborate on achieving an objective. I have many fond memories of these events and will share just a few.

In support of the Prince's Trust in the UK, our team met with a group in their late teens at a local library. These kids had either dropped out of school or left due to some kind of challenge. At the time, my children were roughly the same age, so this really hit home for me. These wonderful young people had the opportunity to talk to us about their hopes and challenges, and we were fortunate to be able to coach them on their resumes or on how to approach finding their path and build their careers. What they needed most was encouragement and a sense that they were valued. It was so rewarding seeing my team interact with the group and make a small difference in these people's lives. We achieved our team-building objective here confident that we had also made a difference for them.

While in Las Vegas at a worldwide conference, I kept my team back for an extra day to work with a local food bank, helping out in the warehouse packing food parcels. While we did not interact directly with the people in need, the story, the help, the teamwork, and the camaraderie we experienced reinforced for me the incredible power of giving as a team builder. I made time at the event to explain why we were doing the work and afterwards to stress what a difference it made.

After one offsite meeting, my team and I took a bus to a local children's shelter that cared for orphans and where children from troubled homes could come for counseling and time away. These children were from homes where one or both partners may have been incarcerated, and I was shocked to find that some ten-year-old kids had never left their neighborhoods before coming to this sanctuary. We helped out in the gardens for the day in preparation for a weekend retreat the shelter was organizing. After the event I asked the team what they had learned, and they shared how humbled they had been by the day and how privileged they felt to do this kind of work. We may come from different back-grounds, but remaining grounded and connected to our communities creates not only a great culture but also a sense of pride that companies like ours care deeply.

An important part of team building and giving programs is the debrief, reviewing the work done and giving people a chance to share what they learned and verbalize their feelings. It is powerful when a team can find their heart in their community and build a passion for more than just work and money. Doing good work is its own reward, but the discussion and debrief after the event can really maximize the team's intellectual and emotional engagement, which is the real outcome you want as a leader.

Reward Trips

The value of reward trips for Sales has been a hotly debated topic in every company I've worked for. These trips normally come in the form of an annual "club trip" where select high-performing employees and their guest are rewarded with an all-expenses paid getaway at a fantastic destination.

Considering the obvious cost of these trips, it might surprise you that the CFO is often *not* the loudest voice calling these outlays into question. It's usually the CEO, CMO, or CRO who object, questioning whether staff members deserve to go on trips for "doing their job." What's more, the optics of other departments that provide vital support to Sales being passed over for these plush rewards can be challenging.

I believe that reward trips serve a vital function in energizing high performers. Plan trip costs into your budget to overcome any fears around internal optics.

Planning Reward Trips

The outcome of a reward trip will largely depend on how you plan and organize it, from setting the criteria for achievement to the location and timing of the trip. Each company will have its own priorities, but here are some things I have gleaned:

1. **Location**: Wherever your team is based, you may be tempted to choose a destination that is "close to home" to save on airfare; just know that this may reduce the allure of the prize. For example, in the continental U.S., Disneyland may not be a favorite if your team already live in Florida or even in the southeast. On the other hand, Hawaii would be a great choice for most. Passport and logistics also play an important role. For example, I loved Bora Bora, but for international staff a U.S. visa was required (if transiting through the U.S.) and it was a long journey. Remember that salespeople need connectivity, even when taking time out, so consider distance not just in miles, but also in time zones for remote locations.

2. **Timing**: I attended one club trip that took place on a cruise ship in the last week of a financial quarter. Somehow it hadn't occurred to the organizer that putting most of our high-performing team on a moving vessel with poor communications at the end of a quarter might be a mistake! I learned that the best time for a reward trip is mid-quarter, usually July or August, as this tends to be a slow time for most companies. Of course, you can plan your reward trip based on your business and/or fiscal calendar and whatever works best for you. In any event, a reward trip planned for six months after the start of your fiscal year can be a great retention tool for high per-formers as well as an effective reset in terms of energy and focus.

3. **Objectives and Outcomes**: While your events team will orga-nize the extramural activities for your club trip, it is up to you to determine the outcomes you want to achieve from the trip. In my experience, the best outcome is a high performer returning home with renewed energy, excitement, and passion as well as with new connections, a deeper sense of team, and a wider perspective on the company and its mission. In most events of this sort, awardees are required to carve out some time for business, so plan to make

the best use of this time. Also, do not underestimate the value of the CEO or CFO making a "guest appearance," even for a day. These small things can add up to the difference between a "free trip" and a true value-add for the individual—and ultimately the business.

4. **Venue Cost**: I have been fortunate to visit some of the nicest places on the planet for club trips. I thoroughly enjoyed these trips, but I had no delusions about the cost. There is a real trade-off between the number of people you can treat and the cost of the venue. I think a good middle ground is a quality five-star hotel with a good mix of activities and amenities. Skipping uber-expensive boutique options gives you the flexibility to reward more people without breaking your budget.

5. **Who Gets to Go**: Staying laser focused on performance, outcomes, and what will build the business is key here. Don't be distracted by other departments lobbying for places. A good rule of thumb is to include employees on contracts that pay sales commissions: If more than 50 percent of their salary is at risk, they should be candidates for reward trips. You may also want to factor in the most important lever in your company's success (e.g., new logo sales). I have seen successful programs that open up a couple of places to supporting functions as a motivation for the whole company. When someone from the Finance deal desk or from Technical Support or Marketing is recommended by successful salespeople, you know that the right culture is being built.

As with all activity in your company, optics are key. Teams thrive on transparency and fairness, so if too many executives make the cut or people without obvious merit start filling spare seats, you should expect your team's energy to change and their trust in you as a leader to be questioned, and not necessarily to your face. Ultimately, these events should drive energy, retention, and performance against stretch goals for the whole company, not just for those who attend.

6. **How Many and How Much**: How many people should attend reward trips and how much should you budget for the entire event? There are many different approaches for reward trips, from smaller companies offering every salesperson achieving over 100 percent a place to larger ones setting a specific number of places for their highest achievers. A lot will depend on your gross margin and where your company is in its evolution. My practice has been to set a specific number, normally between five and ten percent of the sales team, of available places, as long as a minimum sales threshold is attained. Thus, a sales team of 500 would be allocated between 25 and 50 places. (Remember, this will double up with partners attending.) Balancing attendance among different groups is more challenging. For example, Inside Sales may deliver 200 percent growth in small transactions booked while only achieving 110 percent of their plan, where a field rep may book just one (lucky) deal but then deliver 200 percent of their plan. Judging salespeople across different departments with the simple metrics of performance and overall outcome for the company, you will need to build a logical and fair system for determining who to invite and then be able to explain it to the team. After all, you want the people who *do not* receive the coveted invitation to still feel motivated and bought in. To avoid surprises, you should do this long before the end of the fiscal year.

Building an Effective Kickoff Event

The work that goes into building offsite events is huge, and when it comes to kickoffs, it is exponentially greater. Successful events do not happen by accident, and they can often take a year or more to plan.

Location

The first step in preparing for a kickoff is always logistical and will involve the two biggest direct costs, travel and location. As companies grow from a few hundred attendees to over 500, then over 1,000, options become more limited and advance booking much more critical. For events of over 1,000 people, you may need to reserve a venue up to two years in advance. With that kind of lead time, you should also take into account company growth when projecting head count. And don't forget to include supporting staff and presenters in your planning, along with travel logistics.

For most companies with a large U.S.-based sales team, it makes perfect sense to locate your kickoff in a geography that offers easy travel, affordable accommodation, and good conference facilities. As you factor in your international teams, great transport hubs and the location of your HQ will play an important part. San Francisco and Los Angeles are particularly convenient as flights to the west coast are easy to book from everywhere in the world. Florida, Boston, and Las Vegas are other good choices. You may also want to factor potential efficiencies from choosing a venue close to HQ if it is centrally located. This would allow international staff to combine conference attendance with meetings and other useful activities.

Finally, consider the cultural environment when choosing a venue. Las Vegas may be a great solution for global or enterprise companies, given its well-earned reputation for hosting large conventions, but your event agenda will be competing with the city's 24/7 attractions and activities. Well-appointed venues in smaller or calmer geographies without the extracurricular distractions are worth consideration.

Building the Theme

One of the most important steps in preparation for a worldwide sales conference (WWSC) or kickoff event is creating a theme. Great themes are usually simple, on point, and speak to the culture and journey of your teams. For example, when Symantec finalized its separation from Veritas in 2015, the first WWSC theme was "ONE TEAM," something we could all get behind as we rebuilt the team after a massive change to our organization. Another successful theme I used was "Make It Real," which spoke directly to the work we were doing to build our management culture and product set. Whatever your theme, make sure it resonates and becomes a north star for your event and is something you can message with and build into your program. You should finalize your conference theme three to six months before the event to facilitate the best planning. Be careful not to do it too early as the theme needs to be current and something the team can identify with at conference time.

What You Want to Achieve

I was taught many years ago by friends trained in the military that when you address troops and want to achieve an objective, you should boil down your objective into *know*, *feel*, and *do*. Once you have a high-level theme and objective, it is imperative that you define what you want your team to *know* when they leave, how you want them to *feel*, and of course what you want them to *do*. Don't be afraid to be prescriptive here. A good example would be to equip your team to execute on a strategy to make three new customer cold calls per day for their first month back in the office. If you teach them to do this and give them confidence and a plan, you will be surprised at how the team will respond.

We did this by running role-play training with our salespeople on the company's elevator pitch with the goal of giving them the confidence they needed to pitch the company, no matter who they were talking to. We also brought in an expert on demand creation who built a compelling case for how to reach new customers, including the research and process required. During the event, we included presentations from Product Management, sales leaders, Marketing, and the CEO. By the end, the team *knew* their product, *felt* confident in pitching it, and were energized by the strategy. Finally, our guest speaker and I tag-teamed setting up what we wanted the team to *do*: the actions they should take and how they would be measured in the coming months. Not long after the training the results began to flow in.

The Curriculum and Order of Events

I have always relied on great enablement leaders to help me build the curriculum woven into our annual enablement plan, including the platform we use, the measurement we drive, and the overall enablement strategy. Ultimately, what gets done, how it gets done, and when it happens at your WWSC are on you as the sales leader, and your detailed involvement will be critical to ensure that you achieve the outcomes you want.

There are many pieces to consider, including the main conference hall and breakouts, soft skills, technical training, role-plays, competitions, demo booths, regional meetings, manager training, and individual contributor streams.

There will be many voices and many requests for involvement, attendance, and inclusion, but staying on point with the core objectives of your event and what you want your people to leave with must be a key reference point for all these decisions. If you write your core objectives down and make them clear to your colleagues, overcoming challenges or questions with them will be greatly simplified.

I also advise seeking counsel from someone who has done this before. A very basic "wish I had known" was when I saw the costs for "other department" attendees in my first global event. Limiting who can come and why could be the difference between affording demo booths and proper display collateral—or not. You might stipulate that other departments can attend, but only if they pay their own travel expenses. (Good luck trying to recoup that cost *after* an event!) Lean on those with experience and plan carefully.

Figure 17 is a good template for a basic order of events.

Our breakout sessions would typically comprise a mix of three things: product training, teaching your team a high-level pitch so there is one voice for the company, and soft skills like account planning or using the company's mandated processes.

I normally required my teams to complete online training and pass tests before the WWSC in order to maximize the face-to-face time at the event. This training was usually mandatory, with failure to complete resulting in non-attendance and possibly exiting the company. This is serious stuff. Think carefully about what can be done online and then what needs to be taught or reinforced face-to-face.

When Should I Run My Kickoff?

The (short) answer is in the name. Most companies will run their kickoff early in the first month of the fiscal year to galvanize the team and create alignment for maximum momentum. But other considerations may inform your timing:

- **Hiring**: If you have a large ramp in hiring and onboarding of a large percentage of the team won't be complete until several weeks into the new fiscal year, you may want to adjust your timing to include the new cadre of team members.

- **Internal Processes/Quotas**: In the two-plus decades that I've been selling in multinational companies, I've rarely seen quotas delivered to sales reps in time for the kickoff, but when they are, and you can directly connect the plan with the team's ability to win, it creates a very special element to the kickoff that can give you increased momentum. This means close collaboration with Finance and Operations in the run up to the conference, and if official sign-off is not possible, then seek discussion with board members and the CEO to garner alignment on the closest possible messaging you can provide to give the team a clear path to what needs to be done in the coming fiscal. The last element I would consider with regard to timing is product launches. My expectation is that your chief product officer would align launches to key dates, like the new fiscal, but if for any reason there is a delay, then the timing of the kickoff should be reviewed.

Inspiring Leaders

At the beginning of this book, I postulated that inspiring leaders provide a mix of all the elements of this book—a kind of alchemy of *art*, *science*, *inspiration*, and *perspiration* in how they lead and manage—and that long-term loyalty and real leadership are built upon this foundation. I would like to explore this because there is an important theme of inspiration woven throughout the *art* and *science* in these pages. Whether an innate gift or a learned skill, inspirational leadership can unite teams and motivate great outcomes.

Inspiration and Manipulation: Two Sides of the Same Coin?

At a cursory glance, inspiration and manipulation may seem to stem from the same root—the ability to influence others. However, the

High-Level Theme Example	"BREAK OUT"	This would be a theme built for a company about to go through hyper-growth and involves a plan for each department to execute on this, including Sales, Talent Acquisition, Marketing, etc. It would include branding, possible videos, and a strong connection to the call to action for the event.	
Number of days	3/4 depending on roles		
Sun.	Evening	Managers and Technical Staff Arrive	
Mon.		Managers' Session	Technical Session for Sales Engineers
	Morning	Motivational Guest on Culture and Team building	Product Roadmaps
	Afternoon	Building Our Management Culture and Putting It into Practice	Product Training
	Evening (early)	Managers-only Reception to Meet the CEO and Other Execs	SEs Only to Meet CTO and Other Execs
	Evening	All Other Staff Arrive – Host Reception and Welcome	
Tue.		All Staff	
	Morning	Mainstage Kickoff by CRO	
		Mainstage Kickoff by CEO	
		Mainstage Keynote by Guest Speaker	
	BREAK		
		How Will We Deliver CMO	
		Testimonials – Customers and Top Salespeople	
	LUNCH		
		Selected Groups	Selected Groups
	Afternoon	Product Training Breakouts	Product Training Breakouts
	Evening	Community Event and or Team Building Event and Reception	
Wed.		All Staff	
	Morning	Mainstage Kickoff by CRO	
		Motivational Guest on Culture and Team building	
		How to Make Your Plan Number – Finance or other	
		CTO Product and Strategy and Roadmap	
		Selected Groups	Selected Groups
	Afternoon	Breakouts	Breakouts
	Evening	Awards Gala Evening	
Thu.		Regional Group Meeting for Global Teams	
	Morning	Closing Session and Call to Action CRO & CEO	
	Afternoon	Travel Home	

FIGURE 17 Worldwide Kickoff Planning Example

distinction between them is profound. In history, we can see many examples of inspiring leaders who have been wrong, some despite good intentions and others for selfish gain or bad intentions. This "dark side" can be extremely serious. While both inspiration and manipulation can guide people toward particular actions, mindsets, or outcomes, their underlying motivations are poles apart. Inspiration empowers individuals, nurturing their intrinsic motivation and elevating their sense of purpose. It is an authentic drive that seeks mutual growth and benefit. On the other hand, manipulation often operates in the shadows, twisting perceptions and exploiting emotions to achieve selfish ends. While inspiration builds trust and fosters long-term loyalty, manipulation erodes trust, leaving a trail of disillusionment and cynicism. So, while they may both influence behavior, their essence and aftermath place them on opposite ends of the leadership spectrum.

The Elements of Inspirational Leadership

In the fast-paced world of business, leaders come and go, but only a few etch their names in the memory of their teams. These are the inspirational leaders—the ones who uplift, motivate, and leave an indelible impact. While many traits define such leadership, five elements consistently stand out. Let's delve deeper into each one.

VISION: THE LIGHTHOUSE IN A STORM

- What It Is: Vision is the ability to see beyond the immediate horizon and articulate a clear, compelling future. It's the road map that charts out where the company aims to go and how it intends to get there.
- Why It Matters: Without a vision, teams wander aimlessly, like a ship without a compass. A visionary leader offers direction and purpose.

Think of Apple without Steve Jobs or Symantec without John W. Thompson. These leaders not only envisioned a future, they made it palpable, drawing everyone into their vision.

EMPATHY: BEYOND THE BUSINESS METRICS

- What It Is: Empathy is the capacity to truly understand and feel the emotions of one's team members. It transcends professional boundaries, delving into the human side of leadership.
- Why It Matters: Teams are more than cogs in a machine; they're made up of individuals with aspirations, challenges, and emotions. Recognizing and addressing these personal dimensions can make the difference between an engaged, motivated employee and a disengaged one. When leaders show they care, team members feel valued and give their best.

EMPOWERMENT: UNLOCKING POTENTIAL

- What It Is: Empowerment is about bestowing trust, providing the right tools, and granting autonomy. It's the belief that the team, when given the right resources and freedom, can achieve greatness.
- Why It Matters: No one likes to be micromanaged. Empowering leaders understand that their role is not to do everyone's job but to ensure that everyone can do their job to the best of their ability. When team members feel trusted, they take ownership, leading to heightened productivity and innovation.

ROLE MODELING: THE PATH PAVED WITH ACTIONS

- What It Is: A leader is perpetually under the lens of their team, and every action, big or small, sets a precedent. Role modeling is about ensuring that the leader's actions are consistent with their values.

- Why It Matters: Teams look up to their leaders much like a student observes a teacher. Leaders who exemplify the values they expect from their team build trust and encourage the team to emulate their behaviors. Remember, words tell but actions show.

OPEN COMMUNICATION: THE TWO-WAY STREET

- What It Is: Open communication is more than just sharing information. It's about fostering an environment where feedback flows freely, where mutual respect is a given, and transparency is the norm.
- Why It Matters: Teams thrive in atmospheres where they can voice concerns, share feedback, and feel heard. A leader who communicates openly ensures that the team is aligned, misunderstandings are minimized, and mutual respect is cultivated.

The essence of inspirational leadership lies in the subtleties—in the vision that guides, the empathy that connects, the empowerment that elevates, the actions that lead, and the communication that binds. As any veteran leader would attest, these nuances are what create a legacy of inspiration.

Can Inspirational Leadership Be Learned?

The inspiring leader may not be the most gregarious person in the room, nor must they have a "type A" personality. As the book *Good to Great* by Jim Collins showed, some of the greatest leaders were quiet and relatively unknown to the world. Regardless of your own natural talents, it is absolutely possible to learn the elements of inspirational leadership, and while many of those elements are woven into the fabric of this book, I recommend focusing on the following principles:

THE JOURNEY OF SELF-AWARENESS

Every journey starts with a single step, and for an aspirational leader, that step begins within. I remember a time early in my career when I was handed a challenging project. The realization struck that the challenges ahead were not just about external factors but also about my internal battles. Recognizing one's strengths is akin to knowing your north star, while understanding your limitations is about charting the waters you need to navigate. This introspective journey, much like piloting a ship, is pivotal in directing your team effectively. (See Figure 1, The Johari Window.)

CONTINUOUS LEARNING

Just as the landscapes around us evolve, so do the contours of leadership. In my personal journey, ever-changing business dynamics taught me that staying static was not an option. Embracing books, attending invigorating workshops, and seeking wisdom from seasoned mentors are vital. The thirst for learning is what differentiates a fleeting leader from an enduring one.

CULTIVATING EMPATHY

During tenure as a sales leader, I have come to realize the power of genuine understanding. Active listening is not just a skill, it is an art—one of connecting, understanding, and embracing diverse viewpoints. It's about taking that extra moment to understand the person across the table. Because, at the end of the day, leadership is more than just steering the ship, it is ensuring that every member of the crew plays a valuable role in reaching your destination (see section *Listening*).

BUILDING AND NURTURING TRUST

Trust is the silent force that holds a team together. From my early days as a leader, I learned that every promise kept, every consistent action, and even every admitted mistake contributes to this trust. Every action, no matter how minor, either strengthens or erodes this bond.

SEEKING AND EMBRACING DIVERSITY

My tenure in various roles across different regions taught me one invaluable lesson: The real strength of a team lies in its diversity. Surrounding oneself with diverse perspectives leads to solutions that are not only innovative but also holistic. Every unique viewpoint adds another layer of richness to the decision-making tapestry (see section *Global and Regional Differentiation*).

ENCOURAGING INNOVATION

In a rapidly evolving world, innovation is the beacon that lights the path forward. As leaders, our duty is not just to manage the present but to also pave the way for the future. This entails fostering an environment where fresh ideas are celebrated, and risks, albeit calculated, are encouraged. Reflecting back to my times at board meetings and strategy sessions, I've often found that the most groundbreaking solutions come from the most unexpected quarters. The energy in having a plan, in innovating, and establishing a north star is incredibly inspiring.

CHAPTER FOUR

Perspiration, *Not* Inspiration

Getting It Done

For all my thoughts on the balance between soft skills and analytical competence that I have shared in this book, it is all for nought without solid execution and hard work.

One of the mistakes I have made over the years is trying to work harder than everyone else. Maybe this was in part to overcome imposter syndrome. But I like to think it was out of a desire to simply lead by example. While I still hold that leading by example is important, I also know that if as leaders we are not balancing our time in thinking, collaborating, and showing up well rested, we will not be able to command our troops in times of crisis.

When I was a senior leader, my weeks often started on Sunday afternoon, when I opened the CRM system to analyze the opportunities in the pipeline. I'd look at the detail, the momentum, the next steps to win, the activities, and the work each person had done. This was my way of respecting the work the salespeople had done entering data into the CRM system, and instead of relying on reports or asking teams to do more work consolidating information on spreadsheets or in PowerPoint, I reviewed their already hard work and developed thoughtful questions for them. Doing this, I was able to get a real sense of what was happening in deals, but my weekly reviews also reinforced and validated the team's use of the CRM software. (A strong caveat here is that sending messages to team members on a Sunday can result in increased stress for the recipients, so if you do plan to use Sunday afternoon to review your CRM, coach your team to ignore these messages until Monday morning.)

A week in the life of a sales leader can get very complicated very quickly, and establishing what is important and focusing first on your priorities is key. Being able to triage critical but repetitive tasks, priorities or urgent matters that arise, and more strategic priorities will help you organize each week and month into productive sprints.

Meeting with my admin and a core group of trusted lieutenants every few weeks to analyze what was important and plan our areas of focus helped enormously. I often started with a mind map that I initially derived from the book *You're in Charge—Now What?: The 8-Point Plan*[15] to ensure I was covering all the bases, from the board to the customer. I then filtered the process into weekly, monthly, and quarterly cadence and focus, always considering priorities, frequency, and the high-level "what am I trying to achieve" perspective. Time is your single most valuable commodity as a senior leader, and the more you can distill this into focus and sprints, the more successful you will be.

I broke my system down as follows:

Important Weekly Repetitive Tasks

Analytics and Sales Pipeline/Deals Inspection (through a deep review of the CRM system): This is *not* a spreadsheet someone has prepared, but direct interaction with the system and, where needed, questions messaged to the reps in the CRM system. Doing this directly will help you build a relationship with and "know" your sales reps more personally. The insight you get from their responses, attitude, and general feedback should prove invaluable.

Timing: Three to four hours a week for a large organization.

---

15 By Thomas J. Neff and James M. Citrin, Crown Currency, 2007

Forecast Calls: First, with operations and finance leadership for analytics, perceived risk, and a view on what's happening. Second, with sales leaders presenting their forecast (colored by information gathered from ops and finance leadership, which helps with asking the right questions). You may also consider times in the quarter where you seek input from your technical sales staff or others who have contact with the customer to verify your sales teams' data. The old adage "trust but verify" is in play here.

Timing: At least three or four hours per week. (Not for the sales leaders as their time is precious and they should be kept on the call for their section only.)

Account Reviews (generally on Friday afternoons): Give reps one or two days' notice as massive preparation is not required, given that planning for critical accounts should be an ongoing process. In these reviews I would ask reps to come with their manager to present an account plan and explain the strategy and activities planned for the next few quarters. On the whole, I was not too prescriptive about the documents used as some reps found this inhibiting, and I have seen presentations, spreadsheets, and even a customer turn up at these planning sessions. The reps who leaned into these processes were generally the most successful as they saw winning as a team sport and were always looking for help.

Timing: Two hours. Two large account reviews, one hour each.

Forecast Submission Roll-Up: Normally scheduled for the day after teams forecast. Depending on the role in the organization, forecasting may take place on Monday or Tuesday; Mondays for regional managers and Tuesdays for global sales leaders to allow the process to cascade upwards. Field Sales' time should be spent with customers, so run field-level forecasts on a Friday or Monday, leaving their mid-week open for customer meetings and calls.

Timing: One hour to prepare and if needed one hour on a call with the boss.

Staff Calls: Run these less frequently but decide what works for your teams. Consistent communication and ensuring "connective tissue" are massively important for global teams; just keep it relevant and valuable for all and mix it up to include other departments or other agenda items on a monthly rotation.

Timing: One hour to plan and one hour to deliver with the team.

Weekly Sprint Meetings: These work for ongoing focus projects. For example, if hiring is a major focus, take an hour each week to level set and bring key stakeholders together to ensure shared vision and collaboration. These projects, while having a finite timeframe, are important to have on the critical list.

Having a clear picture of the sprints and the activities is essential for a few reasons:

- As your business grows, other senior leaders may circumvent the chain of management, and you will want to know when this happens. Both time and what your team are focused on are important.
- As complexity increases, make sure that the work being done is aligned, shared, and not duplicated to ensure maximum effect.

- Collaborating and having a shared sense of the mission with the team are essential and will fuel the team's energy and sense that they are contributing to something bigger.

Timing: One hour per week.

Prioritized Cadence Activities

Prioritized cadence activities take place based on criticality of the situation. They may include:

a. Performance issues
b. Customer challenges
c. Root cause analysis on issues
d. Decision-making

Calendared Activities

Calendared activities were peppered into my schedule based on our 90-day mind map. My admin was responsible for making sure I covered everything on the map.

a. Country visits / office visits
b. Skip-level calls and brown bag lunches
c. Customer events
d. Annual planning
e. Team events and offsites
f. One-on-one meetings
g. Weekly communications
h. All the meetings and planning from my 90-day cadence calendar
i. Planned thinking time and collaboration time with my inner circle of advisors

j. Planned gaps for rest, travel, or a little down time. I even planned time to walk between meetings as my diary grew so full that back-to-back meetings without a planned gap meant either leaving early or arriving late.

There is never enough time to get to everything. Maintaining a detailed understanding of your situation while having high-level command and control is a delicate balancing act.

I should note here that I have always treated my admins as part of my management team, involving them deeply in running the business and giving them a voice. This is huge, as they have brought real value, not only in time management but in making things happen and also as the "voice of the team." My admins have often had more insight than I into what was going on with the team. I never asked them to break trust in sharing confidences, but they were always able to provide helpful—sometimes powerful—insights, and I trusted their judgment.

"The Ideas Factory Is Closed"

My manager spoke these words as we started one fiscal year. The plans were drawn up, the ideas had been documented, and budgets had been locked. The time had come to execute.

It is important to acknowledge that moment when you move from creativity and ideas to hard, gritty execution, and it may take more than just one conversation or a moment in time to really embed this.

Some time ago, I completed a personality assessment with my team that used colors to illustrate our strengths so that we could work more effectively as a team. Strengths were color coded: green for "operational process oriented," blue for "creative," yellow for "all heart for people," and red for "instruction and orders." I came out mostly green with some yellow, very little blue, and a lot of red when under pressure, but one of my colleagues, whom I valued greatly, was almost all "blue sky." Learning his penchant for creativity helped me realize that transitioning from *ideation* to *execution* may be harder for some than for others, and I was able to adjust my messaging accordingly.

Whether through assessments or another vehicle, it is important to know both your strengths and challenges, as well as those of your team, so that you can better prepare yourself for when you need to step outside your comfort zone. For me, operational focus is my happy place, and learning the different personality types of my team members helped me to adjust my style to help them pivot and focus when needed.

Delegation

Successful leaders understand the importance of not just working hard but also working smart. This involves recognizing one's strengths and limitations. Instead of attempting to manage every task or decision, effective leaders delegate responsibilities.

Select the right tasks for yourself and for your team. Good delegation isn't about offloading only the tasks you don't want to do; it's about identifying the tasks others can do better or more efficiently, allowing you to focus on strategic decisions and high-priority responsibilities. But delegating work is only half the job. Trusting your team to handle tasks—even, or perhaps especially, when their approach and style may be different from yours—and empowering them with resources and autonomy are key. Proper delegation boosts team confidence and fosters a culture of responsibility and growth. Done strategically and thoughtfully, delegation can be an opportunity to learn from others, boost your productivity, and allow people the freedom to express themselves for a great team outcome.

Burnout

When I was a junior manager, we were often coached on managing our time, avoiding burnout, and the importance of balance, including exercise in our daily routine. Until (and unless) you experience burnout, you can't understand how the fatigue and stress affect your health, relationships, decision-making, sleep, and general ability to do your job. That was me, but luckily, just once in my career. I do not recommend it.

It is important to recognize the signs of burnout and act on them promptly. Putting your hand up and asking for help is not a sign of weakness. And especially if a group of people relies on you to lead them, it is incumbent on you to ask for help. This can be challenging, as the symptoms of burnout can make self-diagnosis next to impossible.

As leaders we therefore have a duty of care to be vigilant for signs of stress or burnout in our teams and colleagues. This is especially true given that most people going through burnout are likely to reject feedback or intervention unless it comes from their direct boss. A best practice is discussing this as a team and agreeing on an "early warning system" where team members are supported in voicing any concerns to the boss, and where the boss is fully bought in.

Communication can be challenging in stressful or high-pressure situations. It's easy when times are good and optimism is high, but it is a human tendency to say less or even shut down when conflict arises—the very time when more communication is needed! As a leader you should pay careful attention to the frequency, content, and quality of communication with your direct reports. This will sensitize you to changes in communication levels or levels of sharing—potential red flags for problems that could be early signs of burnout or stress.

I have seen many examples of managers "missing the signal," where someone who left the company had been, in some way, clearly communicating stress or burnout. As leaders it is our job to proactively cultivate an environment of empathy and safety for communication. Even in the best of times, job stress is an unavoidable reality, but by "listening" to what your team is saying (and how they are saying it) while cultivating a culture of trust and candor, you can ensure that they have the oxygen they need to sustainably manage stress.

Grit

In *Grit: The Power of Passion and Perseverance*[16], Angela Lee Duckworth translates the power of passion and perseverance into one word: grit. I was inspired by her teaching and by the simple lessons she gives on how to approach challenges and potential failure.

Sales is not for the feeble-hearted. For all the science, art, and inspiration, it inevitably comes down to perspiration and *grit*, the ability to get back up when you fall (or fail) and press on for the prize.

Having the presence of mind to work smart and focus on the right things is vital, as is leading from the front with an eye for detail while also soaring and seeing the macro view.

I would propose that next to the role of CEO, sales leadership is one of the hardest. The results are binary and easy to see, but the inputs are a complex "system of systems." Ultimately, there is no prize for being second best or for trying hard and failing.

16 Scribner, 2016

The *Perspiration* (or Getting It Done) chapter of this book is the smallest because it is also the simplest: Get the job done, focus on what is important, and remain humble, human, and centered.

Good luck on your journey!

RECOMMENDED READING

Cracking the Sales Management Code: The Secrets to Measuring and Managing Sales Performance, Jason Jordan and Michelle Vazzana (McGraw Hill, 2011)

Grit: The Power of Passion and Perseverance, Angela Lee Duckworth (Scribner, 2016)

Mindset: Changing the Way You Think to Fulfil Your Potential, Carole S. Dweck (Updated Edition, 2017)

Start with Why, Simon Sinek (Portfolio, 2009)

Atomic Habits, James Clear (Random House Business Books, 2015)

8-Point Plan for the First 100 Days, Spencer Stuart

Always Be Qualifying: MEDDIC, MEDDPICC, Darius Lahoutifard (01consulting, 2020)

The Painless Negotiation and other books by Steve Thompson (Value Lifestyle)